To

_____

_____

_____

_____

From

_____

Date

_____

A MOM
After
God's Own
Heart
DEVOTIONAL

Elizabeth George

HARVEST HOUSE PUBLISHERS
EUGENE, OREGON

Cover by Garborg Design Works, Savage, Minnesota

A MOM AFTER GOD'S OWN HEART DEVOTIONAL
Copyright © 2012 by Elizabeth George
Published by Harvest House Publishers
Eugene, Oregon 97402
www.harvesthousepublishers.com

ISBN 978-0-7369-4759-6 (pbk.)
ISBN 978-0-7369-4760-2 (eBook)

Printed in China

15 16 17 18 19 20 / RDS-SK / 10 9 8 7 6 5 4 3

A Note from Elizabeth

Dear Mom,

You spend every waking hour of your day encouraging others. And at the top of your list is encouraging your children, helping them grow up, driving them here and there, and praying like crazy as you watch over their lives. And now, I am offering personal encouragement in this book of devotions written just for you—a busy mom!

In this little book, I've drawn from my own memories as a mom in the throes of child-raising. I've also included my observations gained from watching my two daughters manage eight children between them. From my girls I get a bird's-eye view of the day-in, day-out issues, accidents, and squabbles that occur in every family...right along with the tender, oh-isn't-that-sweet moments.

So please, sit back and relax. Take a minute or two each day to find the strength and comfort you need to keep on keeping on—to hear God's "Well done, My good and faithful mom!"

In His amazing and everlasting love,

Your friend and fellow mom,

Elizabeth George

Let Your Light Shine

🌹

Do you desire that your children love God with all their heart? Then there's something you can do about it. Pray! And put your desire for your children right at the top of your prayer list. Then be diligent to live a life that reveals your love for God. Ephesians 6:4 says to "bring them up in the training and instruction of the Lord" (NIV). There's a very simple way for this to become second nature: *talk* of the Lord. Talk about Him when you're at home and in the car, before the kids go to sleep, and as soon as they wake up. A woman—a mother—who loves God is a light in darkness. Matthew 5:16 says, "Let your light so shine before men [before your children], that they may see your good works and glorify your Father in heaven."

Dear Father, let my lips sing praises, speak requests, and make frequent mention of Your mercy. Give my children ears to hear of Your goodness so that they turn to You, their heavenly Father, with ease and delight.

A Praying Mom

Mom, praying for your children will make a difference in their life. It took me awhile to discover the power of prayer—and I'm so glad I did! As a young mom, I'd made the decision to stay at home. And there were many times when I felt useless and ineffective. But when I was introduced to the idea of prayer as a ministry, that changed my perspective. I began praying *for* my children, *around* my children, and *with* my children. And what a privilege it was to teach my two girls to pray!

Psalm 34:8 says, "Taste and see that the LORD is good; blessed is the man who trusts in Him!" What a blessing—as you cultivate a heart of prayer, you will taste and know that the Lord is good.

Lord, give me a heart of prayer for my children. Allow me to model what it means to go to You with my every need as I teach my family how You extend Your provision, peace, and purpose to Your children.

A Courageous Mom

It only takes a glimpse of email spam to see evil in action in this fallen world. It's more than a little scary. But mom, you can make a difference! Moses' mother, Jochebed, belonged to a sorority of mothers who gave their sons to God to use in the fight against evil. Samuel's mother gave him up for God to use, and Mary saw her son Jesus offered up to die on the cross.

Psalm 37:1 encourages you not to "fret because of evildoers." Instead of worrying or trying to solve every problem in your own power, devote yourself to raising godly children. The power of evil is helpless against the power of the truth you plant in your child's heart and mind. You are a courageous, loving mom when you place your confidence—and your child—into God's care.

God, I receive such comfort and assurance
as I plant Your eternal truths in the heart
of my child. I cannot control the existence
of evil, but I can base parenting decisions
on Your righteousness just as I can place
every hope for my child in Your power.

High and Noble Calling

Lunch out with friends…or quiet time with your Bible? Hmm. Sometimes this choice is really hard, isn't it? Time for ourselves is important, but that priority takes second place to God's calling to train our little ones. This is your highest and most noble calling. But we can't give out what we don't possess, so it's vital to nurture a passion for God's Word and His wisdom.

Spend some time each day reading the Bible. Share its life-giving truth with your children. It requires the sacrifice of time and energy, but the years you have with your children fly by so quickly. Psalm 119:11 says, "Your word I have hidden in my heart." Your time in God's Word is time He'll use to make you a mom after His own heart. It's time well invested!

Lord, help me choose You and Your Word as my source of strength and refreshment each day. I want to deepen my understanding of Your love and Your will so that I become a mother who invests in her faith and family with everything she has and is.

God's Vocabulary

"Time out!" On a bad day, moms frequently repeat these two words to their children. Many moms also confess that they'd love to have a "time out" *from* disciplining children. Yet discipline is definitely part of God's vocabulary for raising children. Proverbs 3:12 says, "Whom the LORD loves He corrects, just as a father the son in whom he delights." Discipline diligently the child you love. And Proverbs 22:6 says, "Train up a child in the way he should go." The Bible teaches that to love your child is to discipline him or her. And Ephesians 6:4 cautions, "Do not provoke your children to wrath, but bring them up in the training and admonition of the Lord." Join with God in the adventure of helping your children to discover, choose, and walk in the right path.

Lord, help me stay the course of raising my children to have integrity, honor, and respect for You. When I want to give in or give up, remind me that raising up a child in Your ways is a privilege. Thank You for Your strength and guidance in this great adventure.

No One's Perfect

My husband, Jim, encourages the men he speaks to with this wisdom: "When God looks at your life—He doesn't look for perfection!" We already know there are no perfect men. Not one! Romans 3:10 says we've all sinned. We've all disobeyed God. The only perfect man was Jesus. Yet are you expecting your husband to be perfect? If so, think again.

Part of being a good mom is being a good helper to your children's dad. Encourage him as he serves his role as spiritual head of your marriage and family. As you support your husband, he is able to more freely do what God requires of him as a spouse and a godly father.

Lord, give me a spirit of encouragement as
I stand by and with my husband. Let him feel
supported and respected in our home through
my actions and words. Give me a desire to
serve the man You are shaping him to become.

A Virtuous Woman

If you want something to aspire to, read on! In Proverbs 31, we read of several virtues that characterize a godly woman. And what a list it is! She is devoted to her family. She delights in her work. She is diligent in her labor. She is dedicated to godly speech. She is dependent on God. She dresses with care. She reaches out to those in need. And she delivers blessings.

Read Proverbs 31 for yourself today. Then take a look at the book of Ruth. It's better than any novel—it's *real* life! Ruth 3:11 says Ruth was known throughout the city as a virtuous woman. Ask God to work the godly qualities in Proverbs 31 into *your* heart and life—that all the people in your town—and your home!—would see that you, too, are an excellent woman.

> *God, I long to be a woman of character.*
> *In today's culture, that is not celebrated as*
> *it is in Your eyes. May others see in me a*
> *heart that is devoted to and dependent on*
> *You for my value, identity, and purpose.*

A Preaching Mother

There are a lot of things we can do for our children—and teaching God's Word is at the top of the list! If you love God and you're a mother, find time in your busy schedule to teach God's Word to your children. It will have value for salvation now and for eternity.

Ruth Graham said of motherhood, "It's the nicest, most rewarding job in the world, second in importance to none, not even preaching." Then she added, "Maybe it is preaching!" Can you see how your role of mom includes giving biblical truth to your children at every opportunity? Take the time and effort to consistently bring God's love and truth to the hearts of your children. It's never too early—or too late—to begin!

Father, give me a passion to teach Your Word to my children—to instill in them Your truth and wisdom. Give me a desire to share a message of faith that moves their young hearts toward You.

Just the Woman

Have you longed for a godly mentor? I've got *just* the woman you're looking for. She fits every requirement. It's the Proverbs 31 woman I'm referring to. She defines what it means to be a woman—and mom—after God's own heart. "She opens her mouth with wisdom, and on her tongue is the law of kindness" (verse 26). This caring mother is teaching her son about women of character. And she wisely encourages him to look for one of these worthy, noble women to be his wife. Are you guiding your son so that he can find a godly wife? Are you inspiring your daughter to become a godly woman? If so, you are becoming just what a good mentor is—a woman who loves and follows God!

God, I am blessed to be the one to share good things with my children. As I tell them about the Proverbs 31 woman, help me make each of her amazing characteristics my own. Help me be this woman!

A Remarkable Woman

Who *is* a woman after God's own heart? And how will you know her when you see her? In the Bible we discover Deborah, who is described in the Old Testament book of Judges as a prophetess, a wife, and a judge. A most remarkable woman, with an equally remarkable calling.

What set Deborah apart as so special? She was an outstanding wife. She sang. She was a poet. She was a godly leader in her home and as one of God's judges over His people.

Deborah lived a remarkable faith in God. Your commitment to God and your heart attitude can match Deborah's. And you have a remarkable calling as a parent. Be diligent. Be devoted. Dedicated. Available. Prepared. Be *remarkable*!

*Lord, give me eyes to see and a mind to grasp
how remarkable my calling is as a mother.
Thank You for entrusting me to shepherd
my children, and for guiding me each step
of the way when I am listening, reading
Your Word, and praying to be remarkable.*

Honor Your Mother

No matter how old and independent you are, God's command is *honor* your mother. The way you treat your mother will model to your children how they are to respect and honor you all the days of their lives. Pray for your mom. It'll impact you both. Speak well of her. Speak politely *to* her. First Corinthians 13:5 reminds us that love "does not dishonor others, it is not self-seeking, it is not easily angered, it keeps no record of wrongs" (NIV). As you treat your mother with courtesy and respect, listen when she speaks to you. Express affection to her with a hug, a squeeze of the hand, an arm around the shoulder. Commit to it! Do it as a daughter after God's own heart and as a mom who wants to show her children God's love in lasting ways.

God, clear away any obstacles I have to
fully, wholly loving my mother. Free me
to be a great example to my children of how
to love their parents. The honor I bring to my
mother and to my children is, in truth, honor
that I also bring to Your precious name.

The Empty Nest

Do you miss the sounds of a full house? Have your children moved on to college, marriage, or their own dwellings? I understand how hard the empty nest stage of motherhood can be. It comes too soon. Hannah, of the Bible, wanted a son so badly that in 1 Samuel 1:11 she vowed to "give him to the LORD all the days of his life." And because she kept her promise, her Samuel had to move to another city. She had to love him across many miles. The mother of writer Elisabeth Elliot prayed and wrote letters. For 45 years she wrote each of her six children twice a week. And that was before computers and email! Reach out to *your* children—and grandchildren—in prayer and love. This investment matters to the Lord and to your family.

God, do I tell my children how much I love
them? I mean to. I intend to. I try to show
it by my care and affection. Help me take
advantage of every opportunity to tell, write,
and share of my love for them…and for You.

A Woman of Good Understanding

The Bible says Abigail "was a woman of good understanding" (1 Samuel 25:3). Now that's something to aspire to! Abigail's very name means "cause of joy." Yet her life was anything but joyful. Her marriage was loveless, for her husband was a harsh man, a drunk. And they were childless. Yet the quality of Abigail's life was faithfulness—to God's Word and to the people in her life.

Whatever your circumstances, you can shine brightly as you remain faithful. Never underestimate faithfulness as a woman, a mother, a wife, and a child of God in the eyes of Your heavenly Father. After all, God is more concerned about us being faithful to His standards than He is about us being successful in the eyes of the world. That's what makes a woman of good understanding.

*Lord, preserve in me a heart that is faithful,
loyal, and loving. I want to understand all
I can about living with joy and perseverance,
no matter the circumstance. When I am low,
lift my eyes to see Your goodness and grace.*

Stranger Love

How did you learn hospitality? Did your mother host friends and acquaintances for dinner? Was your home open to your peers when they needed a safe place to talk and laugh? What a legacy of love that is! Are you sharing that legacy with your children? Hebrews 13:2 says, "Do not forget to entertain strangers." It's been wisely said, "Love has hands to help others. It has feet to rush to the poor and needy. It has eyes to see misery and want. It has ears to hear sighs and sorrows." Pray for a heart that cares, eyes that see, a soul that's compassionate, funds to provide, resources to share, hands that open, and energy to serve. Ask God to work in you and open your heart and home to those in need.

God, please work in me and my heart so
that my home and life are open to others.
Don't let me hold tightly to my possessions or
blessings. I want to become a blessing to You
and to my family. Help me show my children
the way to give, to love, and to have faith.

A Formula for Life

O ne for you...*two* for me." Have you heard your child "share" this way with friends? That might work for children dividing up treats—but as a woman of God, you have to follow a little different formula. I guarantee your life will be better if the priority is God first, others second. Bless and serve your husband, your children, their families, your church, your work—whatever. But always start with God. It's a simple step toward living out God's formula for order in your life. In John 15:5, Jesus said, "Without Me you can do nothing." We need to remember that! Examine your calendar. Does it include priority time with God? God first, others second. It'll change your life and your family.

> *God, if I wander away from Your priorities*
> *for me, give me a gentle nudge back on*
> *track. I know that when I place You first in*
> *all I do and pursue, I am investing in my*
> *and my family's contentment and future.*

Take Care

Take care of yourself—it's part of God's plan for you! When you don't exercise, your back goes out. When you're not careful about what you eat, you lack energy and develop health concerns. When you don't get the proper sleep, you're wrung out for days. I think you get the picture. It's dangerous to neglect your health. After all, there's physical energy involved in living out God's priorities in your life. Nurture your ability to serve your family and God by taking care of yourself with a little extra discipline and planning. The Bible says your body is the temple of the Holy Spirit. And Galatians 5:23 says to develop self-control. It's for your good and for your life, and for your loved ones at home.

Lord, when I replace unhealthy habits with healthy ones, I serve You, my family, and my purpose in Your will better. When I care for my body—this temple of the Holy Spirit—I am honoring Your plan and priorities.

Today's the Day

You see your children growing taller by the minute. You notice another laugh line on your face. It's easy to worry about the passing of time. But don't forget the great gift you have in today! Not one day should be taken for granted or wasted. Do this by asking the question that Micah 6:8 presents: "What does the LORD require of you but to do justly, to love mercy, and to walk humbly with your God?" Pray and ask God, "How do You want me to live today?" How you live now is the legacy you leave tomorrow. Make it your purpose to know what God's will is, and redeem the time for His glory!

Today is the day that You made, God. What
do You require of me? How can this day
be one that is purpose-filled? I don't want
to waste the gift of another day, Lord.

Make the Effort

believe in prayer. I just have such a hard time doing it."
Prayer isn't as intimidating as we think, but like anything worthwhile, it takes effort. There's so much to be accomplished, and prayer is your source of help. James 5:16 reminds us that "the prayer of a righteous person is powerful and effective" (NIV). Let's follow in the footsteps of so many Bible heroes. When Solomon prayed, God made Him the wisest man ever. Elijah prayed, and God sent rain and fire. Daniel prayed, and God locked the lions' jaws. Take heart—the fervent prayer of a righteous woman, wife, and mom accomplishes much! Make Ephesians 6:18 the goal: "Praying always with all prayer and supplication in the Spirit, being watchful to this end with all perseverance."

Lord, I believe in the effectiveness of prayer. I am
grateful that You listen when I lift up my needs,
dreams, and praises. Right now I commit myself
to the practice of prayer with renewed conviction.

Teach Your Children

Wouldn't it be nice if we had an instructional manual for parenting? Never fear, God doesn't expect you to have a teaching degree or even experience! But He most definitely expects you to teach your children. I counted at least 20 times where some form of parental teaching is mentioned in the book of Proverbs. For example, Proverbs 22:6 says, "Train up a child in the way he should go, and when he is old he will not depart from it." No matter what the obstacles, no matter the lack of payoff, no matter how tired you are, or even if your teaching doesn't seem to be making a difference—stay at it! Bringing up your children to love the Lord and serve Him faithfully is what being a parent is all about.

God, You have given me the important responsibility of raising a child. I will not give up! I rest in the promises and guidance of Your Word as I teach my child to love You completely.

Still on Assignment

Are your children grown? Have I got news for you, my dear friend! You're still on assignment. And this is a word not from me, but from God. He says the "older women" in the church are to teach and admonish the young women to love their children (Titus 2:3-4). Are even your grandchildren grown? Well, God is calling you—His older, wiser, more experienced mom—to pass on what you know about raising children. Do you have nieces and nephews? Are there children in your church? Just look at the opportunities you have to be that mature, godly woman in the life of someone younger. You'll discover more benefits to age than you ever thought possible.

Lord, I accept that I am still on assignment.
Lead me to the children! I have so much of Your
love to share with other moms and kids. I want
to be used by You in every season of my life.

Love Your Children

You might be surprised to know how many Christian moms have trouble expressing love to their children. Providing care for our children is God's plan for our life as a mom. It's a way we follow God's pattern of love. I know firsthand how tough it is to dispense TLC when you're busy and things are hectic. And frankly, sometimes children aren't all that lovable! But I had to change my state of mind and heart.

Thank goodness the Bible is the perfect place to turn to for advice. Galatians 5:22 tells us the fruit of the Spirit is love, joy, peace...and what's the next one? Patience! With yourself and with your children. Mom, let your children know you love them. Say it until they believe it!

Lord, I will say "I love you" to my children
when life is hectic or when they pretend
to not be listening. I will keep saying
it...because You never stop saying it.

Training Ground

Home is the training ground for life, one way or another. Proverbs 20:11 says, "Even a child is known by his deeds, whether what he does is pure and right." Open your eyes, mom—what's he or she up to?

Start now to instill the attitudes and actions you desire from your children. And respect is foundational. If your children respect and honor you and your position of authority as their parent, they'll grow to respect all authority, whether at school or as an adult. The Bible promises that their lives will be blessed, and you will be blessed again and again. "Discipline your children, and they will give you peace; they will bring you the delights you desire" (Proverbs 29:17 NIV). Tomorrow's peace begins with the big or small lesson you are teaching your child today.

> *God, when I see my children acting with*
> *respect, I get a lovely glimpse of who they*
> *can become. Thank You for such delights*
> *and for the sweet rewards of parenting.*

God Will Lead You

The Holy Spirit doesn't automatically seal your mouth so you don't overeat—or so you don't yell at your children. But He *will* prompt you! God will gently lead you as you read, study, pray, and try to apply God's Word to every area of life. For example, Proverbs 17:28 tells us that even fools are considered wise and perceptive when they hold their peace and shut their mouths. You have to decide how you're going to respond to issues in your life. Often your best response comes only after you are silent, prayerful, and willing. God's Spirit lives in you as a believer in Christ—and He's ready and willing to assist you with your personal discipline and growth.

Lord, Your peace eases my soul and gives
me perspective and patience. I will follow
Your leading to become an influential
mother. And I will lean into Your strength
to become a wise woman and mom.

Lift Up Your Voice

If you're going to lead others—your children, your sisters-in-Christ, friends, neighbors, or co-workers—on a path of discipline and spiritual growth, you'll have to think of self-discipline as essential and necessary in your own growth. Proverbs 8:1-3 says, "Does not wisdom cry out, and understanding lift up her voice? She takes her stand on the top of the high hill…at the entry of the city."

As you exercise self-control in your life, you will be a model for others to follow. You will cry out and lift up your voice. And your example will glorify God. Others need women who're willing to be a model of Christ to younger women and to their peers. Seek to be that kind of woman. Grow in discipline and you will stand in places of influence—for God's glory.

> *Lord, help me to be a strong example of a*
> *woman after Your heart who lives in Your*
> *strength and gives You glory, who points to*
> *You as my beacon, my light through life. Help*
> *me lift up my voice for Your name's sake.*

Lesser Choices

Is your fire for the Lord burning out? You know what happened, don't you? At some time, for some reason, lesser choices were made and that passion for knowing and following God's plan got lost. If you want to be a woman who lives out God's will for your life, you must first have a passion for God's Word. Be purposeful and willing to stick to God's path. There's so much at stake. Your own spiritual growth, the lives of those you love, your marriage, your witness to others. What you do and don't do doesn't only affect you, it affects everyone and everything. In God's goodness, it's not too late to begin to make good, better, and best choices. God is waiting patiently for you.

*God, please rekindle my flame of faith. When
I first met You, I was hungry for Your Word and
so eager to share it. Today, I will walk forward
with a renewed spark of belief and commitment.*

What's Going On?

❧

"Where is all my energy anyway? What's going on?" These are important questions to ask and answer. When you evaluate your life and health choices, you'll probably discover why you're so tired. What time do you go to bed? What activities are you involved in? Do you have young children? Teenagers? Are you working? Serving at your church? I think you can clearly see what's going on. Something has to give or else something's going to give! And it'll be your body if you don't make changes.

The Bible says Jesus took time to go away and rest a while. If you're going to be that energetic, enthusiastic mom after God's own heart, find ways to build up yourself physically, emotionally, and spiritually.

God, give me discernment to see what
habits need to change and how I can restore
energy and enthusiasm to my life and faith
walk. I want to be healthy, whole, ready, and
willing for each step of my purpose in You.

Start Now

Children! The word sparkles with life and laughter. And lots of energy. And each of them represents a life of potential—for the Lord. Nothing demands that you lean on the Lord more than parenting. Psalm 127:3 says, "Behold, children are a heritage from the LORD, the fruit of the womb is a reward." Teach your children God's Word. And teach them about the Lord all day, every day.

Your children desperately need your diligent teaching and your faithful training. Like all people, children are born sinners and they will develop natural sinful habits and practices. And once those patterns become ingrained, they're harder to correct. Ephesians 6:4 says, "Bring them up in the training and admonition of the Lord." Start now!

Lord, there are many days when it'd be easier to delay teaching and guiding my children. Give me a vision for the heritage of hope and the legacy of love I am sharing with my children each time I instill Your truths in them.

Pass It On

Do you sometimes fret more about the cleanliness of your children's clothes than about the purity of their heart? Well "practical" is good—but not if the spiritual growth of a child is ignored. As a parent, pass on a life of passion and purpose. Not just with what you say, but with how you live. Pray for your children. Be there for them physically, emotionally, and spiritually.

Matthew 6:21 reminds you that "where your treasure is, there your heart will be also." Discipline your children, yet also be their encourager. Make sure their days are filled with words of praise and encouragement—from you! Inspire in them a deep, pure love for the Lord by modeling faith and commitment in your parenting and marriage. The state of their heart depends on it.

*Father, give me eyes that see beyond the material
and practical, and straight to the spiritual
needs of my children. I want to raise them
to know Your promises so that they hold a
reverent, pure love for You all of their days.*

Let It Sink In

You are created in the image of God. Let it sink into your heart that you're creative, intelligent, and a great mom! Every time you reach out in love, perform a kindness, soften your heart in forgiveness, show a little extra patience, or follow through in faithfulness, other people—your children included—experience the character of God through you.

Don't worry about "self"-worth. Instead, rejoice in your worth in God. Don't criticize or downgrade yourself; remember to speak and think the words of Psalm 139:14: "I will praise You, for I am fearfully and wonderfully made; marvelous are Your works, and that my soul knows very well." Today, rejoice in the strength God gives you for each day, and the hope He offers for all your tomorrows.

*Lord, You are my strength and joy. How
wonderful that on the best and worst of
parenting days, I know that I am made
in Your image, and I am wholly loved.*

Love Is a Sacrifice

Love is a sacrifice—a beautiful one, but a real one. Our first baby was every mother's dream. She smiled, and she loved being held. But our second daughter? For the first six months she screamed. Some days it wasn't easy to live under the same roof with her. Yet I kept caring for her, loving her, doing all the things a mother does—as she fought her cholic, writhed, and screamed!

As tough as it is at times, God will help you and show you where you need to exercise sacrificial love. He reminds us that we're to be obedient even when we don't feel like it, because there is a great purpose at hand. Mom, join me in looking to God to empower us to be women who love sacrificially.

> *God, sometimes I am like a child who*
> *cries often—so often that I miss the joy*
> *of sacrificial love. Your tender mercy*
> *calms my spirit and gives me the peace*
> *I need to love my child as You love me.*

Take Joy

Mom, you might not want to hear this, but the Bible says to give thanks—even when you don't feel like it. That's not an easy thing to do, considering what a mom regularly goes through. But it's what God calls you to do as a woman of God. And something wonderful happens when you obey in this matter. When you lift up a heart of gratitude, it's like lifting a diamond to the light against a black background. It enhances the brilliance!

I need God's joy. Daily. And I need it most when I'm misunderstood, or in emotional pain. It's amazing to realize that *you* are your sacrifice of praise, and the very hindrance to your joy becomes the soil in which joy can blossom. Let God comfort your soul that you may know the fullness of joy in Him. Take joy today.

> *God, I thank You for my life, my family,*
> *my children, and my faith. When I find*
> *myself focusing on the difficulties, may*
> *I lift up my gratitude to Your light and*
> *let it cover me in Your radiance.*

A Call to Diligence

Ever feel like running away when life gets tough or complicated? Of course, you can't. But sometimes you do step away from your responsibilities. Yet God says that diligence matters. I love Proverbs because it's an inspirational call to diligence! Proverbs 14:23 says, "In all labor there is profit, but idle chatter leads only to poverty." Why only discuss plans when you can invest effort in fulfilling purpose?

Proverbs also talks about the diligent woman and mom who rises early to take care of the needs of her family, who is strong in her efforts to provide for their needs, who works into the night, who is never idle. And because of this diligence, her children rise up and bless her. Her husband praises her. And ultimately? The Bible says she receives the fruit of her hands (Proverbs 31:31).

Lord, give me a desire for diligence so my
children will learn from it and call me blessed.
I want to invest in actions and efforts that truly
matter so my life. I want to create a life with
my family that is rich in Your abundance.

A Woman of Excellence

I want to encourage you today with some thoughts from God's Word. First, you're known and blessed by God. Jeremiah 1:5 says, "Before I formed you in the womb I knew you." My friend and fellow mom in the trenches, you are loved by God. His Son died for your sins. You are accepted by God. Complete in Christ.

Ephesians 1:3 says, "Blessed be the God and Father of our Lord Jesus Christ, who has blessed us with every spiritual blessing." And most of all—remember, mom, you're a work in progress and will one day be perfect!—Philippians 1:6 says, "Being confident of this very thing, that He who has begun a good work in you will complete it until the day of Jesus Christ." When you question your value or your purpose, seek the comfort of God's promises fulfilled through Christ for you.

Father, I love that You know every part of me. You knew me before my parents did! When I worry about my children or how I am doing as a mom, I can rest in knowing that I am a work in progress. I am Your work in progress.

A Mother's Attire

Did you know that God has a list for His best-dressed woman? On days when you barely get the kids dressed and out the door, it's good to know exactly what you are to wear to please the Lord. He says in Ephesians 4:24 to put on the new person that was "created according to God, in true righteousness and holiness." Put on tender mercies. Put on kindness. Put on humbleness of mind. Put on meekness and longsuffering. First Peter 3:4 says to put on a gentle and quiet spirit. And in 1 Peter 5:5, His faith fashion advice is "be clothed with humility."

When you look in the mirror and complain about how you look, or you compare yourself to someone else, consider how beautiful you are to your heavenly Father. The Bible says God looks on the heart—on the spiritual realities of who you are in Christ!

Lord, I want to clothe my spirit with godly traits. I can be so hurried and harried during the day that I forget how You show me the way to adorn my heart with love, grace, gentleness, humility, and kindness. You call me beautiful.

Remember the Moment

"Do you hear that? The quiet? No one is crying or spilling or arguing. I must be in heaven!" Well, thank God with all your heart for those moments. Enjoy them to the hilt! Sometimes it seems like you'll never get a break, that you're going to lose it. So take notice of the times when your children are charming, delightful, cheerful, and loving. As a mom, you know it can't last. Savor these moments and use them as encouragement on days when you need a boost. I used to write them down in a special notebook. And when I needed a reminder that there were really good days, I'd go to my little book. And I'd remind myself that "being mom" is worth the struggle. One of these days you're going to hear God say, "Well done, good and faithful mom."

Jesus, I find my refuge in You at all times.
Give me an awareness and appreciation
of the times when there is a pleasant
peace in the home and in my heart.

You Go, Mom!

When God said "train up a child"—He didn't leave moms and dads with a vague assignment. He told us in Proverbs 22:6 exactly what our purpose and objective is: "Train up a child in the way he should go, and when he is old he will not depart from it." As a parent you are called to raise your children God's way. And God doesn't leave us wondering what that looks like. Proverbs tells you that the way of the Lord is the way of life, the way of wisdom, and the way of righteousness.

It's your job and joy to teach your children. So instruct your heart out, mom! Live out God's way in front of your kids. Teach God's Word constantly and inspire them with God's wisdom consistently. You go, mom!

Lord, You have provided me with the great opportunity to raise up a child of God. Guide me so that I discipline and encourage in the way of Your truths, promises, and wisdom.

God Is a Finisher

"Life can feel out of control. Sometimes it's impossible to sleep because of the fear." The Bible says God is in control of *all* things. We're not so good at finishing what we start, but God *is* a "finisher." Philippians 1:6 says, "He who has begun a good work in you will complete it until the day of Christ Jesus." When you give your life, future, marriage, children, and job to His plan and purpose, you can live without doubt or fear. For nothing and no one can stop God's good work in you. That's His promise! As a mom after God's own heart, you can offer up a prayer of gratitude for God's powerful promise of completion. Start today by going to the Finisher.

God, You are in control of all. You hold my
future in Your hands and You know the heart,
purpose, and future of my child. Ease my doubts
and fears so that I can walk with confidence
in the gifts of Your promises and provision.

God's Presence

God will help you with *any* difficulty you're facing. How? Just read your Bible—daily. I don't say that casually. The Bible helps you to walk in the way God is directing you. Psalm 119:105 says, "Your word is a lamp to my feet and a light to my path." You will experience such blessing and insight when you watch for and depend on God's light for your every step. God wants you to be courageous as you face whatever life throws your way. Courageous enough to stand up for Christ. To model godly character. To fulfill your role in your family. To speak up for morality at your children's school. To live a consistent life for Christ. You can do it. Not in your strength or power—but with God's character, Word, and His presence!

Lord, give me a heart of courage and conviction. I want to trust Your Word and depend on it as the light that leads me into my purpose and Your truth. Thank You that You show me the way to go with the radiance of Your wisdom and will.

Love Your Husband

I'm going to let you in on a secret about love. Are you ready? Loving your husband really has nothing to do with him, and everything to do with you and your walk with God. Surprised? The Bible calls love a fruit of the Holy Spirit. So why wouldn't it be the highest value for you to love your husband? I guarantee this will revive your marriage! Lavish love on him in the way you prepare a meal, encourage him, speak well of him in the presence of your children and others, and pray over his life.

When you obey God, you'll have all the love in the world to give your husband. Walk by the Spirit and God will do the loving—*through* you! Enjoy every minute God gives the two of you.

God, may I love and honor my husband with
my words, actions, priorities, and prayers.
Your Word and faithfulness show me how to
love my spouse and my children every day.

Loneliness

Moms feel lonely too. Many mothers and wives have days—or even seasons—of feeling lonely. But you are not alone. The Bible says God is with you. It's a fact of life. You will be alone at various times. When your children start grade school, extra activities, college, or their own marriage and family. And most women end up outliving their husbands. But through these times of transition, solitude, and loneliness, you can turn to One who is always there. Pray for and cultivate a firm, powerful sense of God's presence. Then, when you're in physical solitude, you'll realize you're never alone. God promises that He will never leave you or forsake you. And God never breaks His promises. His presence is there *with* you and *for* you. He will comfort and encourage you.

Lord, just when I'm feeling distant from others, I am drawn once again to Your presence. You are my Creator and You are the one constant in my life. You fill me and my days with the joy of Your faithful love.

Going to Church

Do you want to invest in the future? Then take your children to church! This one action will pay dividends for generations. Going to church is just a small commitment of a tiny slice of time each week. Yet this one little practice, over time, makes a huge difference in a life, a heart, and a family. I know that's been true in our family. I didn't become a Christian during my childhood going-to-church years. But I'm so grateful it sowed a seed in my heart that bloomed later on.

Putting God first in a worship setting is a powerful example for your children. Jesus' parents thought it was important to make sure He participated in spiritual worship. Good things will happen because of your commitment.

Father, strengthen my resolve to show my family
what it means to be a devoted person of faith.
I want to model a joyful commitment to the
body of Christ. Give me a heart to pass on to
my kids this legacy of eternal importance.

Teach by What You Do

I have a great piece of advice from a woman who mentored me when I was a young wife and mom. She said, "Elizabeth everything you do and *don't* do—teaches!" Over the years I've applied this truth to prayer and have witnessed its wisdom unfold in my family.

When you pray, you teach your children to pray. When you pray with them on the phone, at the door, as you tuck them in, you teach them to pray. And when you don't? You teach them that prayer isn't important. Let them see and hear your passion for God. And every chance you get, invite them to share about people or their worries to pray about. They'll soon view going to God as the best first response to all of life's situations, needs, and celebrations.

God, give my children eyes to see me pray. Give them ears to hear my praises and petitions. Give them a heart to enjoy the gift of prayer for themselves. Give them a desire to seek You with assurance that You are always there for them.

Just a Mom

I'm *just* a mom! A lot of days, that's exactly how I feel." Have you ever caught yourself saying or thinking that after talking with others who are on the career fast-track? There will be times when you perceive signals that you're a nobody unless you're a woman who works outside the home. And there are those who think your children will make it just fine without your constant care. But I've got a very different take on that. Jesus said in Matthew 6:24, "No one can serve two masters; for either he will hate the one and love the other." Though Jesus was talking about loving God versus loving money, the principle holds up in your choices as a mom. It's not about having a career. Rather, it's about having your priorities in check. The question to ask yourself is which comes first.

God, help me to respect and honor the priority
of raising my children. Remind me of my
worth in Your eyes when I start to question the
value of my choices. I trust Your strength as
I follow the convictions You place on my heart.

Longing for a Lot More

As the wife of a seminary student, I faced real challenges in the area of contentment—and a big part of it was finances! Our family lived in a tiny house with peeling paint and a living room ceiling about to cave in. And all our income was used for tuition, rent, and groceries. Can you relate? Unfortunately, lean times spark a desire for more. But these times become opportunities to give your needs to God in prayer. As a mom you have many concerns to bring before the Father. Let God make it His job to meet those needs and release your desire to have it all right here, right now. Psalm 84:11 says, "No good thing will He withhold from those who walk uprightly." If God doesn't meet it, you don't need it!

God, today I give to You my every need and
want. My heart is full when I realize that
You care about me and provide for me and
my family. Help me show my children what
it looks like to desire a lot more...of You.

Freedom in Christ

I just love the Fourth of July holiday! All the family picnics, children laughing and playing, and fireworks—it's so festive. But its greater significance is the celebration of independence, religious freedom, freedom from tyranny and oppression. As a woman, wife, mom, and grandmother, I'm grateful for the freedom to pray openly with my family, read the Bible without fear, and take a stand for my faith. And just as our country marks its freedom day in history, you have your own independence day—that moment you became a follower of Christ. That's something to shout about! Jesus came so that you might be free. I'm not talking about political freedom, or even the personal freedoms you enjoy, but freedom from sin. Whatever comes your way, remember you have freedom in Christ.

Jesus, I celebrate my independence day! You brought me out of the bondage of sin and into the free land of grace and faith. Your mercy humbles me and instills in me a great sense of loyalty and gratitude.

Priority Living Works!

Do you think priorities are for boring people? Well, I hope to persuade you differently. Just start with three priorities and see how it goes. God: What book of the Bible would you like to read or learn more about? Family: What specifically will you do to serve your husband, children, family members, friends? And yourself: What in your life needs attention, correction, and transformation? Plan to make changes today, however small they may be. Philippians 3:12-13 has an encouraging claim to make your own: "I press on to possess that perfection for which Christ Jesus first possessed me. No, dear brothers and sisters, I have not achieved it, but I focus on this one thing: Forgetting the past and looking forward to what lies ahead" (NLT). There are great days ahead, my friend!

God, Your priorities fill me with joy, dreams,
and direction. What could be more exciting
than that? Your hopes for me are deeper
than the sea and higher than the stars. Let
me experience the adventure of living
Your best for my today and tomorrow.

Happily Ever After

I met my husband, Jim George, on Valentine's Day. I was a June bride! Could anything be more "happily ever after"? Sadly, we began our marriage without God. We argued. We poured our lives into causes, friends, hobbies—you name it. And we had two children, but that didn't fill the emptiness. Eight years went by before we became a family where Jesus Christ was the head. That's when I started my happily-ever-after habit: I read my Bible regularly. I marked every passage that spoke to me as a woman. And God did a makeover on me I'm still in awe of. Matthew 20:28 is the secret! Jesus said, "The Son of Man did not come to be served, but to serve." Eternal joy begins when you love and serve the Lord and your family.

Jesus, when I am tired, upset, busy, or preoccupied with the children, Your grace and unconditional love remind me to return to Your Word. Deepen my desire to be a servant so that I can know what eternal joy is all about.

A Smile and a Hug

Nothing just happens—including a great marriage and a great family life. Take a busy schedule, children, aging parents, a lot of wear and tear, and you have the challenging mix most marriages face. So what are you going to do about it? Proverbs 21:5 says that the "plans of the diligent lead surely to plenty." It'll take effort, but it's worth it. Plan a way to encourage your husband today. Make him feel special. Remind him you love him. Ask the kids to join you in showing their appreciation for their dad's hard work and love. A smile and a hug goes a long way.

If you're thinking, *Hey, what about me?,* well, it has to start with one of you—so why *not* you? Plan a special dinner. Time alone. A regular date night. Celebrate the love you have for one another.

> *God, direct my focus toward my husband.*
> *Let me honor and cherish him by showing*
> *him my love and my gratitude. I want*
> *to be diligent in the way I build up*
> *him, our marriage, and our family.*

Out of Balance

Are you happy? That can be a dangerous question to ask women. Why? Because so often our lives are out of control and our emotions and sense of balance end up spinning out of control too. This happens when we fail to understand God's priorities. But here's good news. A better life is possible! Matthew 6:33 encourages you to "seek first the kingdom of God and His righteousness, and all these things shall be added to you." When God is your priority, time with your husband, children, and others falls into place. Make your time with God a necessity. Second Peter 3:18 calls it growing "in the grace and knowledge of our Lord and Savior Jesus Christ." Your time *is* your life! Now, how do you want to use it?

*Lord, You are my faithful Shepherd. You guide
me toward good and right priorities. Call me to
what matters and show me the way to go. I want
my time to count, to matter, and to honor You.*

Self-discipline

D oes the thought of *self-discipline* make you anxious? Let's examine the idea from God's perspective. His Word challenges and encourages you in this important area. You'll be glad to share about self-discipline with your children, I guarantee it. For example, think about how much hot water you get into because of your mouth. "Whoever guards his mouth and tongue keeps his soul from troubles" (Proverbs 21:23). How about contentment? Proverbs 30:8 says, "Give me neither poverty nor riches—feed me with the food allotted to me." Be satisfied with "enough." Second Peter 1:5-7 says, "Giving all diligence, add to your faith virtue, to virtue knowledge, to knowledge self-control, to self-control perseverance, to perseverance godliness, to godliness brotherly kindness, and to brotherly kindness love." Controlling your actions and reactions isn't about rules…it's about love!

God, give me a desire for self-discipline.
May I respond to my children, others,
and my circumstances in ways that
reflect this godly quality and lead to
contentment, righteousness, and godliness.

Stick to It!

For the inventor Thomas Edison, his first step toward progress was to announce his intentions on a project. Then he'd go into his lab and make the announcement a reality. That's the way to get results—make your intentions known, then ask someone to hold your feet to the fire! A Christian friend. A mentor. A trusted advisor. Even your husband and children can encourage your success.

Do you want to become a more diligent woman of prayer? Do you need to spend more time in God's Word? Do you need to get healthy? Find someone who will help you move forward. Ask that person to hold you accountable to your goal. Then stick with it. Persevere! And Proverbs 28:20 promises that when we are faithful, we will be blessed.

Lord, I want my good intentions to lead to godly living. Give me the perseverance and strength to follow through. Let me be an example to my family of what it takes to keep my word and to live out Your Word.

Hang in There, Mom

Have you had a day filled with driving carpools and assigning time-outs? Of overseeing homework and making sure chores get done? If so, reminding you that children are a blessing from God probably isn't what you need to hear right now! Or—*is* it? Psalm 127:3 says, "Behold, children are a heritage from the LORD." That "behold" is a huge exclamation mark! Children are a blessing and motherhood is a privilege. Setting aside the reality of a bad day, how *do* you feel about your children? Do you cherish them? I'm guessing you do. Sometimes you just need a little reminder. Your children are created in God's image. And you have the privilege of teaching them, training them, loving them, and prizing them! I want to encourage you on the good days and the bad—that as a mom who loves and cares for your children, you are right in the center of God's perfect will.

When I wonder how on earth I can manage,
You remind me to look to You, my heavenly
Father, for perspective, patience, and a growing
capacity to love and cherish my children.

God-honoring Words

What do the people you work with think about God because of *you*? That's one of those "ouch" questions, isn't it? The reality is, when people know you're a Christian, the bar is set higher. What do your neighbors, community members, and children's friends think about God? For that matter, what do your *children* think about God?

"Let the words of my mouth and the meditation of my heart be acceptable in your sight, O Lord" (Psalm 19:14). Are they kind words? God-honoring words? Philippians 4:8 instructs us to think on things that are true, noble, just, pure, lovely, good, virtuous, and praiseworthy. Why? Because what you're thinking about will show up in your behavior—in your words. Maintain integrity of faith in your heart, and the fruit of your life will honor and serve the Lord.

God, I want my words to reflect Your light to others. Give me the wisdom to inspire, encourage, mentor, serve, and uplift my family and others as I also serve and praise You.

The Will to Love

Love is often misunderstood. It's not nearly as sentimental as we'd like to make it. It's really a choice. An act of your will. You're about to leave the office and a client calls with a problem. Or you've just spent the day taking care of aging parents and your daughter's devastated over a broken date. Not exactly a time when you want to invest in someone. Yet that's when you're called to put your will in gear and show love to another. Christian love—God's kind of love—is a deliberate effort, and God gives you the grace to make it happen, starting right in your own home first. John 3:16 brings you back to the most important act of love ever: "God so loved the world that He gave His only begotten Son." This love went beyond human expectation. It wasn't expressed out of emotion—it was an act of God's will!

*God, You are the source of love. When I am
too tired, too agitated, or too self-focused
to extend kindness and compassion to my
family—both little ones and big ones, Your
Word and Your leading guide me back
to the priority of love. Always love.*

Change—for the Better

Like it or not, change is inevitable. Eat all the tofu you like. Exercise, drink lots of water. Stay away from caffeine. But surprise—a common thread in the research done on senior citizens and long life wasn't what they ate or didn't eat. It was their ability to adapt. The group that lived longer did so because they had the ability to change when they experienced a new season in life, the death of a spouse, a different surrounding. You are part of a changing world. Jobs change. Children move away. And sometimes they move back. Transitions happen again and again. The good news is that when God comes into your heart, He gives you a new spirit. Everything changes for the better. Outwardly the circumstances may not be so great, but inwardly… you're transformed.

> *Lord, I want to live like one who is truly transformed. Allow me to see change as a chance to depend on You and rely on Your strength alone. Remove my need to know everything! I trust You, Lord.*

A Great Day—or Is It?

You can plan, schedule, and control—but real life doesn't always go as smoothly as you'd like, does it? Someone's upset with you, the car breaks down, you're in a meeting and the school calls because your child's sick, you get the news your mother has fallen and hurt herself—it's an endless list.

Galatians 5:22-23 says, "The fruit of the Spirit is love, joy, peace, longsuffering, kindness, goodness, faithfulness, gentleness, self-control." As a believer in Christ, you have longsuffering, or patience, as a fruit of the Spirit. Let this verse be a great comfort and reminder when you're dealing with personal relationships, trying to keep a household together, and managing your workday, along with all the other responsibilities you have as a woman. Colossians 3:12 says to "clothe yourselves with…patience" (NIV). It's *spiritual* fashion at its best!

> *Jesus, I want to wear my faith well. Grant*
> *me patience as I parent my children,*
> *encourage my husband, and offer a*
> *listening ear and open heart to others.*

Who Are You Serving?

There *is* time to do everything—but just exactly what is it you want to accomplish? The secret is weeding out the things that don't matter. And that's not easy to do. I love the passion the apostle Paul expressed in Acts 27:23: "God to whom I belong and whom I serve." Who are you serving? As a woman on a mission, start by seriously and prayerfully considering the value of everything on your list and the best time for it. As a mom, you'll always have a bunch of things to do, but until you consider the value of each one, you're merely accomplishing tasks. Make this one change in the approach to your day and I guarantee your schedule's going to look very different. You'll discover God's purpose for the "precious minutes" of your life!

*Lord, present to me a vision for what
I should accomplish. Pare away the
unnecessary pursuits so that I can discern
what is most important in Your eyes.*

What Does Your Home Say?

Wouldn't it be great if your home had the luxurious atmosphere of a five-star hotel? Oh, I'm fully aware you live in the real world—*not* a premiere suite. But what if you transformed your home into more than a place to plop down backpacks, grab a quick meal, and change clothes before heading off to the next thing? I'm not suggesting the perfect home—just a little more loving care that says, "You're special!"

Look at your home with fresh eyes and a servant's heart. Walk through each room and make sure there's a "fussed over" feeling about the space. Pray for the person who sleeps there. Add special touches that let your husband, son, daughter, or guest feel known and cherished. They will hear, loud and clear, that they are loved.

Father, open my eyes to see my home as You do—a place to serve, love, and nurture others. This is a physical space to extend Your spiritual grace. Remind me of this truth every day so I can delight in the gift of making a house a home.

Ten Keys to a Better Marriage

Wouldn't it be nice to have ten keys to a better marriage? Coming right up! One: *Work as a team.* That means leading *and* following. Two: *Communicate.* It takes some practice. Three: *Enjoy intimacy.* God intends that you come together to become a new whole. Four: *Manage your money.* Being content is a start in that direction. Five: *Keep up your home.* Small steps keep a house organized and peaceful. Six: *Raise your children.* Know what the Bible says and agree on a plan. Seven: *Make time for fun.* Laugh together. Eight: *Serve the Lord.* Be prepared for a faith adventure! Nine: *Reach out to others.* Watch for opportunities. And ten: *Grow in the Lord.* The greatest influence on your marriage is your spiritual growth. Matthew 19:6 challenges, "What God has joined together, let not man separate." Amen!

Lord, show me ways to help my husband
and me be a couple of faith and faithfulness
as we serve You, our family, one another,
and others with joy and commitment.

Raising Children

Hmm…what's wrong with *this* picture? You've known parents who seem totally oblivious to the behavior of their little ones. Yet Proverbs 23:13 says, "Do not withhold correction from a child." Teaching, training, instructing, correcting—it's a lifelong challenge when it comes to raising children. And if we don't, Proverbs 29:15 reports the result: "A child left to himself brings shame to his mother." You do your children harm when you fail to correct and direct them. You sentence them to a life of uncontrolled emotions, and all the consequences that go with it. When you discipline your children early in their lives, you are providing them with lasting wisdom, boundaries, training, and skills. Do this faithfully and consistently—with a heart of love!

God, You have seen me give in when I should've been disciplining my child. For the love of my children, strengthen my resolve to not give up on raising them in Your way, Lord.

Teach Your Children

Parenting is such a huge responsibility. It can be scary! Especially when you first bring home that newborn. Or when you barely recognize your teen. But you're more than capable! And the really great news is that you and your husband don't have to do it alone. Psalm 46:1 proclaims that "God is our refuge and strength." Take every opportunity to teach your children about God. Deuteronomy 6:7 says to teach them diligently—when you sit in your house, when you walk, when you lie down, and when you rise up.

Live out what you believe. And be a parent who loves positively. Colossians 3:21 says, "Do not provoke your children, lest they become discouraged." Most important of all, remember your faithful instruction lays the groundwork for your child to accept Christ. "From childhood...the Holy Scriptures...are able to make you wise for salvation through faith which is in Christ Jesus" (2 Timothy 3:15).

God, I depend on You each day for knowledge and energy and conviction as I raise my child. I can't wait for the day when my child comes to recognize You as heavenly Father.

Mom: A Priceless Model

So what's a mother to do? Talk to the Lord about your children! Pour out your heart to Him. Share your concerns. Ask God's help and wisdom—you'll need it. Be a mother who prays—regularly.

If you're married, share your concerns with your husband. Move forward together—two are better than one! If you're a single mom, talk to some older and wiser Christian moms. I can't tell you how important that was for me as a young mother. Even as a married woman, I so desperately needed help and assurance. God put so many incredible women in my path just when I needed them. And as you grow in the Lord, live out your genuine faith for your children. Mom, you will be a priceless model for them.

Lord, I need help. Please connect me with
a woman of God who can mentor me
and remind me that a mom after Your
heart is a great treasure to her child. Lead
me in my walk so that I glorify You.

A Quiet Hero

You can become a hero—one of God's faithful! Recently a friend of mine was part of a panel to determine the national award winner for a volunteer organization that works with abused children. One of the candidates was described by her peers as "a quiet hero" for children. This woman didn't set out to be a hero. She just responded as she always had; she did what had to be done. She was ready when a crisis arose; she was where she was supposed to be; she was doing what she was supposed to do. My dear fellow mom, choose to be faithful! Choose to rely on God's strength. Philippians 4:13 declares, "I can do all things through Christ who strengthens me." Be a mom who serves God by being faithful in all things.

Jesus, I want to be a heroine of the faith.
First for You and then for my children,
family, and community. Show me where
I can make a difference. And give me
the courage to step forward in faith.

Dress Up—
Fix Up—Look Up

Dress up—fix up—look up. Not a bad formula for us gals! *Dress up.* I've always taught my daughters and women I've talked with about personal appearance, to "dress up." Not pretentiously, but appropriately. Why not be a role model to bless others with a pleasing appearance? Set a good example of modesty and loveliness. *Fix up.* What do others see? Someone who neglected to take a little extra time to comb her hair? To look like she cared? How do your children feel when they're with you? Or your husband? And *look up.* Luke 10:27 says we're to love the Lord with all our heart, soul, strength, and mind. Are you consciously aware of His presence? It is His beauty you reflect in your efforts.

Dress up. Fix up. Look up!

Lord, I fix my gaze on You and follow my heart as You lead me. Let me show my children and younger women what it means to truly "dress for success" as I model loveliness inside and out.

Talk About Jesus

My mom rarely talked about Jesus. When I was little, I thought He was a cousin we never saw!" What was your childhood view of God? Point your little (and not-so-little) ones' hearts to God. You tend to talk about what's important to you, so send a loud message to your children by discussing Jesus and praying to Him frequently. It'll make God a part of your child's everyday experiences and conversations. You never know what seeds you're planting in a child's mind that will guide them throughout their lifelong walk with the Lord. Deuteronomy 6:7 reinforces the thought. It says to speak to them of God "when you sit in your house, when you walk by the way, when you lie down, and when you rise up." I think that pretty much covers it, don't you?

Jesus, I want my children to know that
You live with us and in us. May there be
ongoing talk of You and Your goodness
in our home that my children know You
intimately all the days of their lives.

Ten Guidelines for Mom

T en *Commandments*? Well, sort of. Not the ones Moses delivered—but 10 *guidelines* especially for you, mom. Here we go! Teach your children God's Word. Tell them what's right and wrong. See them as gifts from God. Guide them in godly ways. Discipline them. Love them unconditionally. Do not provoke them to anger. Earn their respect by example. Provide for their physical needs. Pass your faith along to them.

It's never too early to start training your children. So whatever you do, do something today. No one—other than God Himself—wants them to walk in God's ways more than you do. You'll need strength, wisdom, obedience, love—and lots of patience. Give Him the glory and step into purpose each day. As Proverbs 3:6 says, "In all your ways acknowledge Him, and He shall direct your paths." My prayer for you is that you will be that mom after God's own heart!

God, I find You to be utterly faithful.
I praise You today for Your unwavering,
unconditional love. Reveal to me new ways
to model Your heart to my children.

Energy to Spare

Have you signed on for one too many committees, fundraisers, or carpools? Are you too tired to think straight? Don't give up yet—you can have energy to spare. I'm about to tell you how, what, where, when... and who! The secret to energy lies in your spiritual life. When you're growing in the Lord, Romans 12:2 says, you renew your mind. I don't know about you, but I can use a lot of that. And right now.

When you read the Bible, you will find yourself seeking the Lord's guidance and strength for every daily task in front of you. Doing this infuses you with energy to work with stamina, purpose, and enthusiasm. The truth is, you were created by God—for God. So it stands to reason you ought to get your energy *from* God. Growth—it's one of God's goals for your life!

> *Lord, I'm too young to feel this old. I long
> to have a zest for life and my family. I will
> come to You and Your Word to be filled with
> the wisdom and energy I need for all I do.*

Number Your Days

You've probably asked several children what they want to be when they grow up. Maybe instead you should ask yourself, "What do I want to have accomplished with my life?" That's a good question to ask at any stage of life. For me, loving and caring for my family is an urgent priority—and one of God's primary purposes for me. But beyond them, how many lives will I have touched? People are one of God's purposes, for in the end, all God will redeem from this planet are the souls of people. How's your marriage? How many women and children are you mentoring? Training? Teaching? How many others are you serving, helping, giving to—and talking to about Christ? Psalm 90:12 says, "Teach us to number our days, that we may gain a heart of wisdom."

God, direct my days so that I use the time
I have to serve You and others. Give me the
sense of anticipation and possibility that
children possess. I want to be a woman of Your
purpose—a woman after Your own heart.

Managing Our Money

Juggling debt each month is throwing off your balance sheet—and your spiritual balance! The problem is, if you're a follower of Christ, what you have is not yours. It belongs to God. Does that mean you are never to spend money on gifts or extras for the kids? No, it doesn't. But you are called to manage your money well.

I so admire the woman in Proverbs 31. She knew a lot about money management. She "sets about her work vigorously…she sees that her trading is profitable…She opens her arms to the poor and extends her hands to the needy" (Proverbs 31:17-18,20). It's a matter of first things first. God's priorities. And it's something that as a mom after God's heart, you need to instill in your children. Then practice what we preach!

God, give me a clear view of Your priorities.
Let me be disciplined and wise with the
resources I receive from You. I want to
teach my children what it means to be a
godly steward of all that we are given.

Your Best Outfit

"All the kids are wearing it!" How many times have you heard this from your children? It's tempting to forego fights over fashion. But mom, this battle does matter. Peek into any classroom and it's obvious that purity isn't exactly in style for clothes *or* behaviors. This is an issue for your daughters...*and* your sons. To raise children who let God's heart shine in their lives, you need to emphasize modesty and self-respect. Let them know that what they say and do will honor or dishonor God. You've heard the expression "Wear your heart on your sleeve." Well, the woman in Proverbs 31:25 wore God's heart on her sleeve: "Strength and honor are her clothing." Show your kids what it means to live a life of style that honors God.

Lord, help me to guide, insist, and persist in the matter of modest appearance and attire. Grant me a positive way to present this so my child understands how clothing reflects character.

Help!

"Where does the time go? How can I handle all the important things in life?" Are you crying out for help, my friend? There are many needs to fit into your limited hours. Time with God. Time with your husband. Time with your children. Time with family and friends. Time for yourself—like *that* will happen any day soon! Time for the unexpected—that will definitely happen! The unexpected part, that is. Time for shopping. Time for baking, wrapping, and shipping. How can you manage it all? There are days when it's hard to get your arms around the concept. But stop and remind yourself—it's all about priorities. God's priorities for your life. God is to be your ultimate priority. And the rest will fall into place.

God, in Your goodness, You make it easy
for me to prioritize my life when I come
to You first each day and place You first in
my decisions and actions. Thank You.

Freedom...and Discipline

"Kids need the freedom to grow and be kids." I couldn't agree more with this statement—but growing requires freedom and discipline. And discipline has lost a lot of its luster in today's lexicon of child rearing. It's hard to grasp, and even harder to follow through—but parents do their children a disservice when they fail to correct and direct them.

Proverbs 3:12 says, "Whom the LORD loves He corrects, just as a father the son in whom he delights." God says to you as a mom, "Discipline your children, discipline early in their lives, discipline faithfully and consistently, and discipline out of a heart of love." Count on it—your kids will protest, cry, squirm, and argue. So? While a child may cry, as Solomon said, "he will not die" (23:13).

Lord, give me Your perspective of what my child needs. I want to give my children a godly, amazing future—a future that starts right now and requires my diligence.

What's It All About?

If you're a mom, laziness just isn't part of the picture! You're running, struggling, balancing, discovering, mending, crying, laughing. Take heart—and take up God's calling for you. Maximize every opportunity to teach your children about God and to raise them with His priorities and principles. Do your best and trust God with the results. Live out what you're teaching. That's what being a mom is all about.

Colossians 3:21 says, "Do not provoke your children." And remember, your faithful instruction lays the groundwork for your child's salvation. The Bible says you're to teach your children God's Word, His precepts, and His values—and you're to do so *diligently*. What could be better than seeing your child embrace the Savior?

Jesus, give me a clear vision of how to invest in my child wholeheartedly with the perseverance and hope of a godly mom. Let this be my child's heritage!

Life Is Brief

Time goes so quickly. That's never more evident than when you're watching your child grow up. The Bible says that life is brief. Like a vapor. A shadow. There are simply no guarantees! It's why you need to put the most into each 24-hour day by loving your family, helping as many people as you can, and giving as much as you can. Your home, your ministry, your job, your *minutes* must be relished and used wisely and fully. A wise mom doesn't want to waste precious time when it comes to her children. In the book of Proverbs you learn that fools squander, waste, and fritter away their time and their lives. You are made by God for God—He has a purpose for you. And that should give you new energy, new direction! Grasp God's plan and purpose for your life.

Lord, with Your strength, direction, and grace,
I am creating memories of a lifetime. I am
set on creating the best home and future for
my children. Let me not waste a second!

Not Feeling the Love

More than a billion Valentine's Day cards are exchanged each year. And yet a lot of moms aren't feeling the love. Sadly, love is a quality often misunderstood. It's easy to confuse it with a physical desire for your spouse or a lavish covering of praise by your children or friends. Yet those versions can occur without any feelings of real love or affection. God's kind of love is as different as day is from night. God's kind of love isn't selfish, conditional, or self-gratifying—it's directed toward others. The Bible says in 1 Corinthians 13:8 that "love never fails." But loving requires an act of the will. A choice to love your neighbor, your husband, your children, your enemies. Examine your heart. Is there ample evidence of God's love?

Lord, I must be honest. Sometimes I don't feel loved. And I base my worth on false versions of what love is. Grant me a giver's heart so that I love others without conditions or expectations...beginning right under my own roof. Grant me Your heart, Lord.

Principle for Peace

I f you've caught yourself whining right alongside your children, you're struggling with a real problem, my friend. Grumbling is an easy habit to fall into. I'm so thankful for the woman who shared this "principle for peace" with me: "The wife and mother is to be the thermostat in the home, not the thermometer." Like it or not, you set and maintain the atmosphere under your roof. If your emotions rise and fall, your family feels it. You can be a blessing to your husband and children by maintaining a peaceful home. Ask God for His peace to rule your heart and mind, and you'll notice changes for the better. John 14:27 would make a great framed verse for your home: "Peace I leave with you, My peace I give you."

Jesus, today I'm exchanging my complaining for Your pure joy. This is who I want to be! Give me a steady peace so that my family comes home to a calm refuge of security and love.

God's Purpose

You can own a fancy GPS system and still not know where you're going—in life, that is! Fortunately, God has a unique purpose just for you. He has a purpose that's common for you as you call Him Lord and Savior. Romans 8:29 says you're to be conformed to His image. If you're married, God's purpose for you is to love and respect your husband. If you're a mom, His purpose for you is to care for your children and train them spiritually. And at all times, His purpose for you is that you be His witness. Pray for a vision of God's purpose. Understand His unique plan for you. Then you'll never lose your way.

God, I desire a sense of purpose so badly.
I ask for Your leading and conviction. I'm
excited to fulfill Your purpose for me as a
mom, a wife, and a woman of faith.

Change—It's Good for You

I f your life is clouded by boredom, then this is your day to embrace the gift of change! When you're adapting to new people, new ideas, a new ministry, or a new calling, it helps to set your sights on God's future. Life has many different seasons, and as a partner in marriage and in parenting, you have to adapt. Your little ones won't be that way for long. Your teens will grow out of the phase they're in. Whew! God's specialty is transformation. We're in good hands all the way. Second Corinthians 5:17 says, "If anyone is in Christ, he is a new creation; old things have passed away; behold, all things have become new." God has not promised you status quo. He promises a new heart, a new spirit. Rejoice in the remarkable gift of possibility!

> *Lord, when I settle for less than You have*
> *for me and my family, convict me so that*
> *I awaken to the gift of beginnings, changes,*
> *and possibilities that are born of Your will.*

Intentional Prayer

I don't need a regular prayer time. With two small children, I'm in a constant state of prayer—usually beginning with, 'Lord, help me!'" I totally understand this, and I'll bet you do too. But I guarantee your life and your parenting will run a lot smoother when you keep a regular prayer time. It eases your soul, soothes your spirit, and will bring you that help you need.

This intentional prayer time doesn't have to be long—but make it a specific appointment in your busy schedule. It's a privilege to pray for others, to pray around the world for God's people. And then with the psalmist you can claim Psalm 66:19 with confidence: "Certainly God has heard me; he has attended to the voice of my prayer."

Sweet Lord, I will come to You with intention each day with my offerings of prayers and praises. I want to have a thriving, regular, and ongoing dialogue with You, God. You sustain me. You know me. You hear me.

Your Spiritual Battery

Every mom will experience some especially long days. And there are a few stages of a child's development that are especially draining. A little battery recharging never hurts. Especially if you're a mom with young children. It's one thing after another! I'm so pleased and grateful that church groups are making moms a priority for Bible study groups and nursery services so a busy mom can take a break. At whatever age or stage of your life, spiritual growth is important.

Psalm 51:12 offers a refreshing way to call out to God: "Restore to me the joy of Your salvation, and uphold me by Your generous Spirit." Call out to God for His joy and generosity. It will bless and recharge not just your "mom life," but every area of your life. You'll even have moments to bless others—to bless your children, your husband.

Fill me, Lord. Recharge my spirit with Your lasting joy. You are my source for all strength, power, and grace. To Your heart I will return again and again for my daily renewal.

Small Changes

You won't believe what small change adds up to. And I'm not talking about your coin jar, although that's a great example of this devotion's message. I've written an entire book about "small changes"—learning to put them into practice so I could be the best mom and wife, the best woman I could be. The book of Proverbs shows the wisdom of what my mom put into practice—and passed along to me. Proverbs 9:1 says, "Wisdom has built her house." Proverbs 14:1: "The wise woman builds her house." Proverbs 24:3-4: "Through wisdom…the rooms are filled with all precious and pleasant riches." And Proverbs 31:27: "She watches over the ways of her household." "Home" has to be "built" and watched over. It takes a lot to make that happen. But God's Word makes it clear that it is also essential and doable. Start small and believe big!

God, let me start today with small changes that lead to big blessings for my household. When I try to do it all in my limited power, remind me to let You shape my life, bit by bit, in Your time.

Making a Change

A woman who resigned as the director of women's ministries at her church told me she did so because her priorities were out of order. She said, "I find it easier and more rewarding to minister to the women at church than to take care of the needs of my children and my husband." And you know what I say to this woman? Good for you for recognizing the misplaced priorities and making a change.

What's important is not what the women at church think of you, but what those at home think of you. Ephesians 5:22 says "Wives, submit to your own husbands, as to the Lord." God is the one you are to please and honor. And you do that by aligning your priorities with His. Determine what you need to add and what you need to pare away to be a mom, wife, and woman of spiritual integrity.

Jesus, You don't ask me to run all over town and say yes to every commitment. You ask me to run straight to You and say yes to Your priorities. I already like this way of living better!

Raising Children Is a Challenge

"My children are out of control! Maybe we've been a little too lenient with them." If this has been your realization, then this strong message from the Bible is for you. Proverbs shouts to every parent that if you fail to discipline your children, it's the same as hating them. But when you correct your children appropriately, you're following in the footsteps of your heavenly Father. Children need to learn wisdom and understanding so they'll grow and mature and become responsible adults.

You hurt your children when you allow them to live without guidelines or consequences. They need it all. Teaching. Training. Instructing. Disciplining. Sounds like a challenge, doesn't it? It's what being a parent after God's own heart is all about!

Lord, I'm up for the challenge of correcting
and guiding my children. I want to see
them grow up to be whole and faithful
adults. Lead me so that I may follow Your
instruction as a loving, caring mom.

Mothering Is for Life

Mothering is for life! I hope that's good news. Being a mom means spending a lot of time on your knees before God. Talk to the Lord about your children. Share your concerns and feelings of inadequacy with Him. Ask for His help and wisdom. Purpose to be a mother who prays. When I was a young mom it was so helpful to have older and wiser women as my advisors. I sure needed their help! I also needed their grace and understanding. Like the older women in Titus 2:3, they taught me how to love my children.

One of the greatest privileges you'll ever have is bringing your little—and big—ones to Jesus. Jesus said we're to do just that. Matthew 19:14 is where Jesus said, "Let the little children come to Me, and do not forbid them; for of such is the kingdom of heaven."

Jesus, turn my feet, my eyes, my words, my thoughts, and my every motherly instinct toward Your will and purpose. I want to lead my children to Your embrace and the rewards of a lifelong and eternal relationship with You.

What's the Message?

Some moms face their child's teen years with a defeated perspective. "They'll do what they want anyway." Giving the power to make decisions to your teen might temporarily calm the battle over what they wear and how they behave, but it isn't a lasting solution. And it isn't the right message.

What message do you want to send? Whatever you do, it's God's beauty that is to shine through your efforts. And then, as Matthew 5:16 says, He is glorified. Make your life statement one that reflects God's standards. Adorn and carry yourself in a way that honors Him and speaks well of Him. It's about sending a message. Setting a lasting example for your children in every aspect of life is more important than making life a bit easier in the moment.

God, I know the battle is worth it. The discussions, boundaries, rules, and the discipline are how I demonstrate my love. I pray that I will avoid the easy temporary solution and remain focused on the eternal.

Your Choice

God never forces you to live a godly life. It's a choice you make. You have to decide if you will or won't obey God's prompting in your life. He doesn't seal your mouth so you don't yell at your children. He does, however, gently lead you as you read, study, pray, and seek to apply God's Word to every area of your life. Do you struggle with a temper? With temptation? Proverbs 25:28 says, "Whoever has no rule over his own spirit is like a city broken down, without walls."

Spending time in God's Word is an act of discipline, and it is also a forever-act of learning, discovering, and connecting with God and His leading. How are you going to respond to the issues in your life? I highly recommend that you choose to go to God first.

Lord, You hold onto me through the storms, the mistakes, and the times of brokenness. I will respond to all that mothering and life present by seeking Your direction, choosing Your love always.

A True Leader

If you consider yourself a leader and no one's following you, think again! If you're going to have influence on anyone else—if you're going to give godly wisdom to all who care to listen—you have to embrace discipline as an essential and necessary part of your growth. You can't lead others, your children, your family, your friends down a path of righteousness you haven't personally taken.

It takes *self*-control before your life can be a model for others to follow. Proverbs 8:1 says, "Does not wisdom cry out, and understanding lift up her voice?" With self-discipline as a guiding principle, you'll be able to cry out and lift up your voice. And others who are watching will listen. They'll learn from you, a true leader. And they will glorify God with you!

*Father, guide me in Your wisdom so that
I am a godly woman of influence. May
I, my family, and those who choose to
follow Your will form a parade of praise in
Your name. May we lead others to You.*

The Theme Is Diligence

Diligence. It doesn't exactly stir a whoop from the crowd, does it? You probably associate it with discipline and drudgery. But guess what? Diligence is a major theme throughout the Bible—especially in the book of Proverbs. Listen to this: "The hand of the diligent makes rich" (10:4). Or how about Proverbs 14:23? "In all labor there is profit, but idle chatter leads only to poverty." Staying with something until it's finished—like being a great mom—takes work and persistence. The Bible also tells us that the diligent woman wraps herself with strength from God's Word; that she receives the fruit of her hands; that her own works praise her in the gates; her children rise up and bless her. How's that for a whoop?

*Whoop! I will celebrate diligence, Lord. I desire
spiritual strength and faithfulness. As a
mom, I want my children to call me blessed
and to see my disciplined faith as a blessing.*

We Can't Say Enough

Modesty? Purity? How about just plain old appropriateness? Unfortunately many moms set the standard too low for themselves and their children. The Bible says in 1 Timothy 2:9 to dress yourself modestly. Note it doesn't say ugly, unattractively. Modesty is simply a lack of excess. That's not too common these days, is it? And I'm not just referring to young people. Proverbs 31:30 gets us back on track. The Bible says, "Charm is deceitful and beauty is passing, but a woman who fears the Lord, she shall be praised." A woman focused on praising God, on honoring Him in every area of her life, will consider carefully how she's dressed because her heart will dictate both her wardrobe and her appearance. Enough said? As moms, we *can't* say enough!

> *Father, I am Your daughter. I will watch*
> *how I dress, how I present myself and You*
> *to others. I will also teach these principles*
> *to my children. Let me focus less on*
> *charm and beauty and more on You.*

Love Your Husband

Another Elizabeth—Elizabeth Barrett Browning—wrote these now-famous lines in one of her poems: "How do I love thee? Let me count the ways." Well let's count a few, shall we? And let's focus on your husband. First, make the choice to love him. Often it starts with that. No excuses, no putting up roadblocks. Just do it. When we choose to love our husband as God has commanded, we bring glory to the Lord. And you're to love him ahead of your children. That's a tough one for many moms, but it's the priority God has established for a family.

Loving anyone consistently and thoughtfully is difficult. But it's a choice we make. Stay in God's Word. Ask Him to help you in this area of love. Make it a priority to love your husband. Then let *him* count the ways! Your children will be blessed by the love you show to their dad.

God, bless me so that I may show love to my husband with great affection, care, and respect. Remind me to nurture this relationship—the foundation for my children's lives and our home.

Being a Godly Parent

You've probably put a lot of time and attention toward making sure your children are pursuing quality activities—but too often the list isn't complete! What about going to church, memorizing Bible verses, learning how to have daily devotions, how to pray, how to give, and how to serve others? Your role is to point your little boys and girls to the Savior—to introduce them to Jesus. And it's an awesome privilege. This doesn't mean they can't be involved in other things—just don't let the other things become the priority.

Loving your children and teaching them God's ways is what being a godly parent is about. As 1 Timothy 6:12 says, "Fight the good fight of faith, lay hold on eternal life, to which you were also called and have confessed the good confession in the presence of many witnesses." Your children's hearts are at stake!

Lord, I come to You eager to be a godly parent, to be filled with the encouragement and vision to fight the good fight of faith on behalf of my children and their salvation.

A Model Home

Home is a place where *people* live. That's obvious, right? Or is it? I love to look through model homes. I can enjoy looking at the layout and be as critical as I want because no one actually lives there. It's all assembled like a movie set—but no one's home. There's no heart, no life activity, no laughter, sorrow, spilled milk, or leaky faucets. By contrast, your home has people. And God has charged you to nurture your family.

The woman in Proverbs 31:13 is said to have worked "willingly" in her home. A labor of love. King Solomon, the wise master home builder, wrote in Ecclesiastes 9:10, "Whatever your hand finds to do, do it with your might." So do your thing and make a home!

> *Lord, give me peace in place of stress, and*
> *belief in place of doubt. I want my*
> *service to my family—our home—to*
> *be a true labor of love. I am blessed.*

A Model for Teens

Jesus' life as a young boy is an incredible model—one you can share with your teenagers. When Jesus was 12 years old, his parents found him in the temple courts, sitting among the teachers, listening to them and asking them questions. God expects you and your children to develop your minds. I encourage you to help your children develop a positive attitude toward learning—at school and in the study of God's Word. Colossians 3:23 says, "Whatever you do, do it heartily, as to the Lord and not to men." How's that as a poster for a teenager's room? Take advantage of every day, every opportunity to learn and grow. Good decisions give you the freedom to choose greater opportunities—no matter what your age or stage of life!

Jesus, when I worry over how to introduce my child to godly wisdom, I forget that it can be as simple as introducing them to You and Your story.

The Lord Is My Shepherd

The Lord is my shepherd." Those opening words of comfort from the twenty-third Psalm are a reminder that God cares for you. He is your personal Shepherd who will be with you through every joy and challenge of life.

You may be a woman who needs that message right now—a woman whose children have turned their back on your counsel; a woman who's raising children alone; a woman facing a life-threatening disease, financial struggles, or an unhappy marriage. Whatever your circumstance, you are a woman who is loved and cared for by the Shepherd. Repeat it with me: The Lord *is* my Shepherd—and because of Him, I will not be in want!

My Shepherd, when I am lost, You look for me
and lead me home. When I am hurt, You bring
me comfort. You meet my deepest need—my
need for a loving Savior. Thank You.

He Leads Us

My heart goes out to every mother, wife, husband, son, or daughter of someone who is missing their loved one who serves in the military. It wasn't that long ago that Jim and I stood with one of our daughters and her children at Pearl Harbor as our son-in-law was deployed. Those moments of panic and worry—and good-byes—can be overwhelming. But in such times we can turn to the comfort of God's presence and promises.

I often think of those words from Psalm 23: "He leads me beside the still waters." Or John 14:27: "Peace I leave with you, My peace I give to you…let not your heart be troubled, neither let it be afraid." God promises you will find that much-needed peace of heart and mind as He leads you to the calm, still waters of His peace, assurance, and unconditional love.

Lord, You lead me and You know the way
ahead even when I cannot see beyond the
step in front of me. Your peace is my refuge.

A Fierce Love

Family. Think about how deeply you love and care for them. How concerned you are about each precious life under your roof! As a mom, you worry and struggle right along with your children. What they do impacts every part of you. I know how that feels. It's a fierce love and protection moms have for their children. You want to protect them from anything that will hurt them. It's the same with God, the Good Shepherd.

Jesus said in John 10:14, "I am the good shepherd; and I know My sheep, and am known by My own." It is Jesus who leads you, who brings you to still waters, who offers you love and care and concern. God knows you. And He knows the hearts and purposes of your children. He will not let go of you or them when the path is rocky. He loves you fiercely!

Good Shepherd, when I fret, You beckon me to the calm and balm of Your care. Thank You for guiding me and my family, for loving those whom I hold dear with an incomparable passion.

Set the Standard

I t's like our kids have taken over our home!" I remember
all too well when Jim and I were up to our elbows in
child-raising and the peer pressure on our girls was creating serious challenges for our family. Jim and I were
never legalistic or overly demanding, but we did set
standards for our family. As our head-of-household, Jim
was responsible and accountable to God for loving and
leading us in the right direction—in God's direction.

Whether you have a husband who is leading you or
not, you have a voice in setting standards for what takes
place in your home. As Psalm 23:3 affirms, God guides
us in paths of righteousness. Set the standard—*God's*
standard—for your family and home.

> *God, thank You for giving us a way to raise*
> *our children to have integrity, faith, and*
> *respect. When parenting feels futile, You*
> *direct our hearts and renew our convictions.*

In Your Face

❧

Maybe you can name a woman in your life who seems to delight in your failures, who gets great pleasure out of getting in your face. When I think of difficult people, I never fail to think of Hannah's situation in 1 Samuel 1. She was totally pushed around by her husband's second wife. In fact, she was *persecuted* by this rival for her husband. This "other woman" taunted Hannah year after year, laughing at her because she hadn't had any children. But in God's presence, there was rest. After her time with God, Hannah felt restored and replenished.

My friend, what circumstances cause you to feel alone or unloved? A child's difficult behavior? Another person's harsh comments or judgment? Do as Hannah did. Seek your true friend—God. Open your heart to Him who loves you completely. Delight in His friendship!

*My Lord, replenish my spirit. Sometimes
I feel so disconnected, so broken. I come
to You as my friend and Savior—You give
me rest and restoration that is lasting.*

We Need Hope

Can a person live on hope? As you face a very uncertain future, I believe hope is *exactly* what you need! Hope that only God can give. You can hope in God's continued goodness. Psalm 23:6 says, "Surely goodness and mercy shall follow me all the days of my life." And what is that goodness? It's all the attributes of God together.

Do you carry a big burden right now? Whether it's a sick child, a lost job, an aging parent, a teenager out of control, God knows right where you are, my friend. Rest in this wonderful insight from Psalm 100:5: "The LORD is good; His mercy is everlasting, and His truth endures to all generations." When you need His strength for whatever life throws at you, God will be there. And that truth will be there for your children and their children. Hold tightly to the hope of the promise of God's continual goodness and mercy!

Lord, I'm holding on to Your goodness with every bit of strength I have. Your mercy is a sanctuary that I and my children can come to forever. You, my Lord, are so good.

For Your Teen

❦

This devotion is dedicated to the teenager in your house! Would you take what I'm going to say and pass it on to your teen? It's so important. You may have already talked to your child about purity. If not, *please* do! I'm talking about sexual purity. God makes it very clear in His Word that He wants you—and your children—to be pure in body. First Corinthians 6:19-20 says, "Your body is the temple of the Holy Spirit...you are not your own...glorify God in your body."

Be sure that your growing child understands purity is more than just saying no to sex. It's about what is put into a body as well—whether intellectually or physically. It's all about choices—about choosing to do what's right and pleasing to God. First Timothy 5:22 says it so simply: "Keep yourself pure."

God, help me with my personal purity. And help me create an open dialogue with my child so that I can speak Your wisdom in a way that it will be heard and embraced.

Your Checklist for a New Life

Today *can* be the first day of the rest of your life—it's up to you! And to get you going in the right direction, here's your checklist. Are you ready? Start each day with God. In God's Word. In prayer for yourself, your day, your family, your attitude, your walk with God. Do all things to the glory of God. That means where you work, with friends, with your children, in whatever ministry you're involved. Each day choose to live for Christ. Live by walking in the Spirit. Live by making right choices. Ask God to help you stay committed, to experience what the apostle Paul meant in Philippians 1:21: "For to me, to live is Christ, and to die is gain." God will bless your faithfulness as you trust in Him. Then follow Him—with all your heart!

Lord, I live too much in the past. I bring regret with me wherever I go. I'm ready to believe in and step forward into the future You have for me. Today is the first day toward this hopeful journey, and I'm excited!

Actions Speak Louder than Words

It's been said—and wisely so—"You teach little by what you *say*, but you teach *most* by what you *are*." To teach and encourage other women, including your daughters, to be what God wants them to be, you have to be what God wants you to be! Thankfully, Titus 2:3-5 gives you God's outline. We're to be dignified, not malicious gossips, self-controlled, teachers of good things, lovers of our husbands, lovers of our children, discreet, pure, lovers of our homes. These are the traits you're to have yourself, and essentials you're to pass on to others—your girls first.

Doing the good things you're supposed to do and being what you're supposed to be is how you become what Titus means by a teacher of good things" (2:3). Be a mom who embraces this incredible calling of God!

Jesus, make me aware of my actions and what they "say" to my child. I want to be a good and wise teacher. Let my legacy be honor, compassion, and integrity.

Love Your Husband

Do you sometimes lament that your love life is lackluster? That's why wives need to know what the Bible means when it calls us to love our husband. When Titus 2:4 says to love your husband, it's referring to friendship love—a willing, determined love that's based on God's command and not on a husband's worthiness. That puts a whole different spin on things, doesn't it? It's the kind of love you show to a friend. Obvious love. Observed by others. It's demonstrated by how you speak to and treat your spouse. And the way you speak *about* him when in the presence of your children, friends, and others reveals the condition of your heart. This active love is a conscious decision you make! How will you love your husband today?

God, I get so caught up in life's responsibilities
and my duties as a parent that I forget to
show my husband the kind, thoughtful love
of a friend. Help me to treat him as my best
friend, with this respect and tenderness.

Most Important Lesson

Are you taking advantage of every opportunity to teach your children about Jesus? I hope so. It's foundational for their lives, and yours! As a mom you have so many chances each day to plant God's Word deeply in the minds and souls of your children. You just need to make use of those opportunities.

Ephesians 6:4 reminds you to bring up your kids in the training and admonition of the Lord. But you cannot give to them what you don't possess. That's why you must nurture a passion for God's Word and wisdom. Make the Word of God a "first place" kind of thing in your home. Pray with your children. Read the Bible to them. Memorize verses together. The assignment to nurture your children never ends. And the most important lesson never changes: Jesus.

Jesus, do I introduce Your ways to my children enough? Give me clarity to see every opportunity I have to teach them that Your love and salvation is for them personally.

What's First?

How does a mom choose priorities for her kids? School events or church events? Family time or study time? It isn't easy!" As a parent, I get that! But once you establish guidelines with your kids, the dilemma will fade away. We constantly reminded our two girls that their priority was family first. Don't get me wrong—we attended a ton of school activities. And we encouraged our girls to bring their friends to church events. But Jim and I tried to apply "good, better, best" to our family activities, putting family first by taking them to church. And we did our share of driving and picking up and dropping off at all kinds of activities both at church and school. God is your willing and able partner as you raise your children to know Him, love Him, and serve Him—to put Him first.

Lord, give me a sense of priority as I teach my children what matters most. Help me show what it means to build a life of faith and love for Jesus.

The Extra Mile

If you're a mom, you've gone the "extra mile" more than once—and that's just *today*! Matthew 5:41 says, "Whoever compels you to go one mile, go with him two." And that certainly applies to your family doesn't it? Let's face it. You have to be a mother to your children and you have to do all that goes with that—so why not go the extra mile and make it special? Ruth Graham made Sunday the best day of the week. There was always some kind of activity or outing in the afternoon. It was the Lord's day, a day to rejoice and be grateful. Do whatever you need to do to make life wonderful, fulfilling, and unique. Those mundane tasks of daily life—the first mile—are great opportunities for adding on and celebrating the extra mile!

*Jesus, fill me with inspiration and spark my
creativity. I want to think beyond routine.
I want to quit settling for less than special.
I want to be a "more mom" each and every day.*

Favor with God

Have you ever wondered what kind of woman God chose to be "blessed among women"—to carry in her womb the baby Jesus, to love Him as her firstborn son, to raise Him in the knowledge of the Lord God? What kind of woman did God choose to be the mother of His precious, only Son?

In Luke 1:30-31, an angel came to Mary and said, "Do not be afraid, Mary, for you have found favor with God. And behold, you will conceive in your womb and bring forth a Son, and shall call His name Jesus." Mary was young, poor, inexperienced, and unaccomplished. Yet she was obedient! And God chose her to be the mother of Jesus. Do you want to do extraordinary things for God? You can start by loving and obeying Him.

Jesus, I'm saying yes to You today.
I choose to follow You and Your Word
with a heart of obedience and as a
mom, woman, and child of God.

Called to Teach

God is calling on you to share what you know—to share with your daughters and granddaughters and other young women God brings into your lives. Who will it be? The young girls in your church? Or a teenager you know? Don't you think they'd welcome an older friend? A lot of teen girls are looking for help, for answers to the questions they don't always ask their parents. And don't forget the college students, singles, newly married women, and new moms.

God understood how important relationship is to the learning process. Your faith and wisdom are not meant to be kept to yourself. There are others who need you to teach them, to encourage them. Is your heart open? Are you ready? Hey, you'll do great!

*Lord, show me who to connect with and
how to do it. I don't always feel like I have
something to offer. Guide me in this
important role and give me a genuine desire
to encourage and teach other women.*

Give Love

First John 4:8 says, "God is love." And He calls you to walk in that love, to love one another, to love your spouse, your children, your neighbors—even your enemies. I can't think of a better gift to give than that! Where is God placing you right now so you can show your love by your actions? For example, how are you responding to children who won't obey? To a relationship that isn't what you want it to be right now? To not feeling well? Love has work to do, doesn't it? And you know what you need to remember? Love isn't based on how you *feel*. Rather, it's based on the grace of God. You are to *give* love!

God, my day is filled with opportunities to extend love to others. Help me to show and tell my kids, husband, and friends that I am grateful for them, proud of them, and that I love them.

Better than Good

It is nice to be considered a good person. But God is calling you to become something more—a woman of noble character! Start with the Word of God. Titus 2:3 says you're to be a teacher "of good things." Think about it: You are to teach good things, virtuous things, to other women and to our children. And you do it by example, by setting a high standard for your conduct. To do that, you have to be what God wants you to be: Dignified, not gossips, self-controlled, a lover of your husband and children, a lover of your home. In other words, a good woman! It's all about the way God wants you to live your life, the relationships He wants you to have, and the character qualities He wants you to pursue—to His glory.

> *Lord, words like* dignity *and* self-control *are*
> *rarely used anymore. But I want these traits*
> *as a noble woman of godly character. Let*
> *me follow and praise Your better-than-good*
> *standard of living, loving, and believing.*

An Ultimate Treasure

If you own three Bibles but haven't opened any of them in a while, you still don't have God's Word…in your heart! And you're missing way too much. Psalm 119:11 says, "Your Word I have hidden in my heart, that I might not sin against You." That's powerful language. The Bible keeps you from sin. It'll also lead you in the right direction. Psalm 119:105 says, "Your word is a lamp to my feet and a light to my path." I find that pretty comforting! Wherever you are, mom, you have the light of God's wisdom to show you the way. Hebrews 4:12 says the Bible is living and powerful, a discerner of the thoughts and intents of the heart. My friend, the Bible is your ultimate treasure! God's Word is more desirable than gold, and sweeter than honey.

*Lord, I want to treasure the treasure of Your
Word. I need its riches for every aspect of
life. And I want to share its wealth of wisdom,
promises, and hope with my children.*

Not Enough Time — Ever

When you say you need more time, maybe it's the actual managing of your life that's the problem. Well, good news. You can learn how to better manage your life. The truth lies in priorities. They aren't just options; they're life-determining. For example, time with God. How much of a priority is it? What about time with your husband? Time with your children, your family and friends, the work you've committed yourself to do? And time for yourself? You need to refuel and spend time connecting with God.

Second Peter 3:18 says, "Grow in the grace and knowledge of our Lord and Savior Jesus Christ." What *are* the priorities that determine how you spend your time? Adjust them and be sure they are aligned with God's desires for you.

> *God, shape my priorities to fit Your will and*
> *vision for my life. I want to invest time and*
> *energy in things that matter and are a part*
> *of Your big picture. Give me a willingness to*
> *let go of anything that isn't Your priority.*

A Dynamic Life

Schedules, planners, calendars...help! I want my life to be more dynamic than that!" Believe it or not, a dynamic life takes a whole lot of planning. Let me amend that just a bit: A dynamic life *with God's purposes in mind* takes a lot of planning! A schedule also helps you live out your purpose of serving God and fulfilling His desires for your life and your day. And, too, if you don't set aside time to nurture your relationship with God, there'll be no bold life—no dynamic life!

In Acts 27:23, Paul spoke of God as the One "to whom I belong and whom I serve." I guess it boils down to that, doesn't it? To whom do you belong? And who do you serve?

Jesus, I love my family and the many activities
we participate in. But I want to be sure
I am serving You with my time and my
commitments. Lead me to make space for time
with You first. Lead me to a dynamic life!

You Can Have More

Do you long for more? More life? More purpose? You can have more by taking one simple step: Start praying over the potential of your day. Pray over your day, through your day, and at the end of your day. This intentional, ongoing communication with God will provide you with His clear direction. With it, you will be open to opportunities or others. And you won't waste God's golden minutes on the foolishness of this world.

When you turn to Philippians, you'll discover one of the most practical books in the Bible. In chapter 3, verse 14 Paul says, "Press toward the goal for the prize of the upward call of God in Christ Jesus." Pray. Make your plans, and as 1 Corinthians 14:40 urges, "Let all things be done decently and in order."

Lord, open up my day to all You have for me
to experience. I will gladly trade my busyness
for Your abundance as I press on for the goal of
"more." I want to start with more of You in my life.

Talking and Listening

Anyone with children knows that unfortunately, talking and listening aren't always synonymous with communicating. Has this been your experience too? Thankfully, the Bible gives some expert counsel on communicating. Proverbs 15:1 says a soft answer turns away wrath. Proverbs 16:24, pleasant words are health to the bones. Proverbs 10:19 says, "In the multitude of words sin is not lacking." Boy, isn't that the truth? And James 1:19 says, "Be swift to hear, slow to speak, slow to wrath." Pay close attention to the tone of your voice, to the words you use. Proverbs 16:21 says that "sweetness of the lips increases learning." Learn to communicate—God's way—as a mom after God's own heart!

God, adorn my speech with uplifting,
helpful, wise words. Let what I say be
worth hearing. And give me a patient ear
to hear the needs, wounds, and hopes of my
family with a tender, loving willingness.

Make Marriage a Priority

The best way to build a more godly marriage and a stronger foundation for raising your children is to continually grow in the Lord. It's your Priority #1. Your spiritual growth will change you! And it will change your relationships with your children and your husband. A nurtured faith will produce wisdom to encourage and listen to your husband. Just for a week, act upon these suggestions. First, pray and ask God for wisdom. Then pray again! Respect and honor your husband. Invest time in your marriage. Realize marriage is a book with many chapters.

Make your marriage a priority. And enjoy your husband! Enjoy God's gift of marriage. In this, you also honor the Lord.

God, increase my knowledge and
understanding of Your ways. I want to extend
Your unconditional, attentive love to my
husband. Together we can show our children
and one another all about Your grace.

What a Savior!

When you hold your child, do you see his future? Her purpose?

Mary's little baby Jesus was the long-awaited Savior. He came to take away the sins of the world, including the sins of Mary. In Luke 1:47 she says, "My spirit has rejoiced in God my Savior." This mother loved her child, and she loved her Savior.

Do you need a Savior? Do you currently enjoy all that the word represents—forgiveness of sins, assurance of heaven, freedom from Satan's power, a relationship with God through His Son? If not, name Jesus your Savior right now. Pray, "Forgive my sins. Come into my heart, Lord Jesus." And whether you've belonged to Him for a minute or a lifetime, when you hold the truth of the Savior, you are looking at your future.

Lord, my love as a mother toward my children is so miraculous and tender. The love I have for You, my Savior, is even sweeter and deeper. I hold onto Your truth as You hold onto my heart forever.

Great Plans

Can women have it all? Most women want to cry out, "Yes!" But while aiming for "all," many miss the mark of God's plan. God has great plans for you, no question. And He will do great things in and through your life. But hold firmly to your foundation in Christ. Make sure your priorities are in order in every pursuit.

If you're a working mom, do everything you can not to miss the privilege and opportunity to train your child—yourself—in the way that child should go. You're creative; you can find ways to make this happen. I have no doubt about that. When you want to go on a guilt trip, don't. Instead, ask God for His wisdom, His strength. Philippians 4:6 says, "In everything...let your requests be made known to God."

Father, search my heart and see if my goals and dreams are the ones You have shaped just for me. Show me how to make my children's upbringing my priority and my passion.

A Frazzle-free Zone

Have you seen this woman? She's got *everything* under control! No fits. No stomping or slamming. No grumbling. Who *is* this woman? Well, it's not always me! But it's who I *want* to be. More like Jesus. More "under" control and less "in" control. I don't know one woman who isn't constantly dealing with stress. Whether it's balancing work and home, children who don't behave, or community commitments—there's always a list, isn't there?

The solution? You have to learn to live a godly lifestyle in the whirlwind of your life. To walk through each day and each trial with balance, calm, and a frazzle-free head and heart. Impossible? It seems like it. But the answer is to look to God's Spirit—the Spirit whose fruit in your life is gentleness, meekness, and self-control.

Oh, to be like You, Jesus! The control and
strength You offer is beautiful...even tender.
This is the frazzle-free, faith-filled woman
I want to become, a woman after Your heart.

Teach Your Daughters

love being a mom. But at times, my girls are more challenging than I am wise!" I can relate to that. As the mother of two daughters, I took their teaching and training very seriously.

If you have daughters, it's important for you to teach them to be godly women and to value a godly home. I enjoyed praying with my girls, memorizing Scripture with them, and going to church together. We had our share of problems and attitudes. But we stayed at it—for their benefit and for their future. And now we have sons-in-law who are so glad we did! Proverbs 1:8 says, "Do not forsake your mother's teaching" (NIV). Where better could you as a mom put your efforts and your energy than in your children—for the cause of Christ in their lives and hearts?

> *God, when parenting challenges arise, let*
> *Your wisdom rise up in me. And may*
> *Your discernment replace my uncertainty.*
> *Growing faith in Christ in my children*
> *today is the most important thing.*

Children Who Love and Serve

As a mother and now a grandparent, I truly enjoy talking with other moms. I love discussing God's calling to be a godly woman and a loving mom. No one can love your children like you do, and to do that, you can follow five God priorities: (1) Make loving your kids your highest pursuit. (2) Search God's Word for guidelines for being a loving Christian mother. (3) Watch the older Christian women as they express Christlike love. (4) Look to an older Christian woman to teach you the how-tos. (5) Learn from these women.

You are not meant to parent alone! Godly women and the gracious Lord will help you leave your mark on the world by leaving behind children who grow up to love and serve the Lord.

*Lord, You encourage me as a mom by
connecting me with wise women. You teach
me Your priorities through Your Word. And
You place on my heart the privilege and
burden to raise godly children. Amen!*

Who's #1?

A marriage's success depends on more than *finding* the right person—it depends on *being* the right person. That's getting personal! It's easy to forget the emphasis Genesis 2:18 places on the role of being your husband's helper. Jesus said He came not to be served, but to serve (Mark 10:45), and you are to do the same, for the sake of your spiritual growth and for the well-being of our husband.

And what if *he* doesn't follow this teaching? It's no excuse for you not to! I know it's hard, but trust the Lord. Instead of objecting or demanding, try making your husband number one. He is to be second only to God in your allegiance and loyalty—even a higher priority than your children. It's not a question of submission to your husband; it's a question of submission to God!

God, I am convicted today in my heart.
I have been very focused on my needs and
wants and have ignored the chance and
responsibility to serve my husband. Help me
to change my attitude and behavior today
out of my love for You and my partner.

God's Little Blessings

"Children may be a blessing from the Lord, but this morning my 'little blessings' were making me wonder about that!" I remember those days all too well. Let me tell you, it's great being a grandmother!

The Bible says your children are a blessing from God. Psalm 127:3 calls children a heritage from the Lord, a reward to be prized. They're created in God's image—that's why they're so special, so priceless. You may complain and moan and groan about your little "blessings," but that's exactly what they are! And you are to teach your children, train them, love them, and prize them. Lavish them with your love. It will work wonders in your children's hearts and lives—and yours too.

Lord, I am blessed to have little hands to reach
for my own, little smiles to brighten my morning,
little spirits to nurture in Your love, and little
reminders that You are good, so good to me.

Parenting 101

Parenting 101—let's go back to the basics! I don't know where you are on the parenting scale—one child, or a house brimming with children. Or maybe like me, you're up to round two and you now have grandchildren. There have been many child-raising techniques taught over the years, but there are certain 101 core values and guidelines to always keep in mind. It helps to know and believe that children are a good thing, although some days you may wonder!

Pray for your children. And your grandchildren. Take them to church. Love them. Teach them. Deuteronomy 6:7 says to teach your children God's Word, and to teach them diligently and daily. Train them, guide them, befriend them. I once saw a poster that says, "What is a mother? She's a woman who prays for her children!"

Father, You are my model of parenting. You are
the giver of grace, patience, discipline, wisdom,
guidelines, forgiveness, and so much more. Today
I lift up my children to Your care and I vow
to be a praying mom all the days of my life.

Make a Plan

Schedules are easy to write up, but a lot harder to live up to. Whether you have one child or four, it can seem impossible to follow a schedule! But don't forget to have a daily schedule and a routine. It'll be a lifesaver for you. Start with the basics: schedule meals, naps, playtime and playdates, baths, and bedtime. Be sure the Bible is a part of your children's everyday life, too. Read a bit of it aloud and say a short prayer together. Then stay on track as much as possible. Give yourself grace as you adjust to the day's plan. There are so many distractions, and *not* having a plan in place just makes it worse! And please—schedule a time just for you to be in God's Word. It will refresh you to take on any schedule.

God, help me to help myself and my children
by starting a schedule and a routine. The
stability, security, and godly habits I create
today will shape my child's future.

Willing to Be Willing

No price can be put on God's will! No paycheck or income or benefits from a job or a career can ever substitute for living your life according to God's will. And God's will is revealed in God's priorities. To nurture your relationship with your husband is at the top of the list. Then to love and care for your children. Those are priorities over any profession. As a busy woman, you have to make difficult decisions to maintain what you know is the right thing to do, and I applaud you for doing that!

Psalm 33:11 says, "The counsel of the LORD stands forever, the plans of His heart to all generations." No matter what society tells you to want, as a woman after God's own heart, you want what God wants. Ask Him to make you willing to be willing!

Jesus, I seek Your counsel today as a mom,
wife, and woman of God. I long for clarity
and passion so that I walk in priorities
that I know come from You. Don't let me
settle for anything less than Your will.

Give It All to God

Worry seems like a job requirement for motherhood, doesn't it? But there is an alternative. Philippians 4:6 says, "In everything by prayer and supplication, with thanksgiving, let your requests be made known to God." Trust God with *everything*. Everything? It sounds impossible, but it's God's promise that you can trust Him—and your choice to do so!

Whether it's a conflict at work, problems with a child, difficulties in a marriage, or feelings of anger—you can give it all to God and trust His ability to help you. What a difference it'll make in your heart, your life, certainly in your marriage. Ask God to strengthen your faith in His readiness to help you. Honor and glorify Him in every circumstance of your life!

God, You know how stubborn I am and how greatly I need Your comfort and help. I give You all my concerns for myself and my family. Let Your name be praised as my anxiety is replaced by Your peace.

Supernatural Boost

You have mega responsibilities and wear a dozen hats. And if you're like most moms, you're always tired. I'm way past that stage in life and I'm *still* tired! But Jesus' words in Matthew 11:28 are a balm for us: "Come to Me, all you who labor and are heavy laden, and I will give you rest." I'm immediately in rest mode when I read and remember this. The Bible says that when you cast your burdens on the Lord and wait on Him, you mount up with wings like eagles. You run and you're not weary (Isaiah 40:31).

Your load isn't going to get lighter anytime soon, but you will have that spiritual, supernatural boost from God that will have you soaring with joy. And dear mom, get as much rest as you can so you can enjoy the benefits God has for you!

What a delight and comfort You are to me,
Lord. You call me to Your presence to soothe
my soul and revive my spirit. You replace my
weariness with energy for today. Thank You!

Surprise Yourself

Do you avoid trying new things because you're afraid to fail in front of friends or family? Who says you're going to blow it? You'll never know unless you take a leap of faith. You might surprise yourself and others! Imagine leading that Bible study you've always wanted to do? Or heading up a committee? Or making a presentation at your children's school? Sure, you might get nervous. And it's good to be prepared. But eventually it comes down to making the "sacrifice" of trust so you can experience God's peace and His confidence.

Isaiah 9:6 calls God our Prince of peace. Imagine leading that Bible study or making that presentation without a worry in the world. God's in control. You can trust Him for the outcome. Now *that's* God's peace for a mom after God's own heart!

*Jesus, I lean into Your strength today so that
I can walk forward in a purpose without
fear and with Your peace. I'm excited
to be a woman of God-confidence!*

Marriage Takes Time and Energy

Just like anything else you value, it takes time and energy to make a good marriage. Jim and I have tried to follow God's way and His leading as husband and wife and as parents. And although we certainly don't have all the answers, I can pass on what we've learned: First, work as a team. Learn to communicate with each other. And while you're doing that, remember Proverbs 15:1: "A soft answer turns away wrath." Enjoy the intimacy you have as a couple. Manage your money. Keep up your home. Raise your children to honor God and His Word. Make time for some fun—it's so important! Serve the Lord. Reach out to others. And by all means, choose to grow in the Lord—together!

Father, when I seek Your guidance, You fill my
relationships with integrity and intimacy. May
my husband and I honor Your good name
as we build a strong marriage and family.

Loving Correction

Do babysitters dread getting a call from you? Even if others don't have issues with your children's behavior, do you? It's time to put your foot down...on the solid ground of God's teaching. Proverbs 13:24 says those who spare the discipline spoil the child. Proverbs 3:12 states, "Whom the LORD loves He corrects, just as a father the son in whom he delights."

Don't withhold loving correction from your children. When you fail to correct and direct your kids, you fail *them*. When you hesitate to discipline, you're choosing a life for them of foolishness, pain, and often harsh consequences. Discipline early, faithfully, consistently, and from a heart of love. Yes, they will protest, cry, whine—you know all the buttons they push! But don't let that deter you from doing what you're called to do as a mom.

God, I want to raise kids who honor
me, their father, and You! Don't let my
timidity or tiredness keep me from doing
right by my family. When others speak well
of my kids, let me praise Your name!

Be a Wise Parent

You don't have to sit your children down and have a long, deep discussion in order to share wisdom with them. Just use every small, daily opportunity to teach them about God. In Deuteronomy 6:6-7 God said, "These words which I command you today shall be in your heart. You shall teach them diligently to your children, and shall talk of them when you sit in your house, when you walk by the way, when you lie down, and when you rise up."

As a wise parent, do your best and trust God with the results. It's the best counsel I can give you. And Proverbs 22:6 promises when your children are old, they will not depart from it. Be sure you live out what you teach. Remember that your faithful instruction and the way you live has a bearing on the direction your children take in life.

Lord, every bit of understanding and
faith I extend to my children today is an
investment in their future. Help me to better
my behavior so that I give my children a
living example of godly wisdom and grace.

Practice What You Preach

believe actions do speak louder than words. And I'll bet that your child believes the same. Your children have a front-row seat for watching how you treat others, invest your time, and handle hardship. They won't listen to you preach something you don't practice. Living a genuine faith in front of your children is key to their spiritual attitude toward God.

Your authentic faith gives you a platform and credibility when you teach God's Word to your kids. If you want them to love and follow God, they have to see you doing that same thing. Proverbs 27:23 says, "Be diligent to know the state of your flocks, and attend to your herds." Like the Good Shepherd who knows and cares for His sheep, you are to know and care for your children.

Good Shepherd, guide my steps as I live
out Your truths with might and integrity.
Let my children see what it means to
live an authentic, active faith.

Creating a Legacy

Sheri's one of those remarkable women who quilts. And her quilts are beautifully and lovingly crafted. Anyone would be proud to own one. But for Sheri, the best part of the experience is not the compliments she receives. No, it's the joy she derives from sharing her love and skill for quilting with her granddaughter. She is doubly blessed because now she gets to see the lovely quilts created by her granddaughter. And as these two work on their creations together, there's a young lady learning to love the Lord, "just like grandma!"

I can't think of a better metaphor for a mom's life and ministry than the beautiful patterns, textures, and "sewing together" that a quilt involves. What legacy of faith are you creating for a child today?

Jesus, You took time to sit with children and share Your joy with them. I want to follow Your example so that a pattern of grace is woven into every moment I share with my children.

Seeking God's Wisdom

At one time or another—maybe even right now—you will be in a circumstance you never imagined would happen, bad or good. Are you prepared?

As a mom your life is complex and demanding. And if you're a woman with the "mind of Christ" as Scripture so wants you to be, you live out many God-given roles. You need as much of God's wisdom as you can get! Proverbs 2:6 says, "The LORD gives wisdom; from His mouth come knowledge and understanding." And it's there for the taking. Are you seeking it? Reaching for it? Immersing yourself in it? Living it out? If there is anything in your life that holds you back from adopting the mind of Christ, it is time to let it go.

Lord, I lift up my trial to Your capable hands.
I need You and Your wisdom. I can't see beyond
this circumstance, but You see from here to
eternity. I rest in Your all-knowing wisdom.

Matter of the Heart

Busy moms need quick access to God's peace! Take time today to meditate on Proverbs 4:23: "Keep your heart with all diligence, for out of it spring the issues of life." Read it until it settles in your heart. After all, doing things God's way is a matter of the heart. It's true in how you manage your time, your resources, and when it comes to how you raise your children.

Your heart is the mind, the thoughts, the motives, the desires of who you are. And your actions come from that place. And as a mom, your job assignment from God is to raise children after His own heart—children who seek to follow God and hopefully experience salvation through Jesus Christ. It's all about fulfilling God's instructions to you, dear mom.

> *Lord, I want all that springs forth in my*
> *thoughts and actions to represent Your*
> *way. I will hold Your Word in my heart*
> *and let it guide my steps and decisions as*
> *a mom and woman of genuine faith.*

Start Here

Maturity in faith has to start in God's Word. Plan a time that allows you to make God your sole focus. What about a schedule for you and your children to have a daily Bible story time? It'll become your shared journey of devotion to God.

Are you taking your children to church regularly? Make it a day they look forward to. Memorize verses with your children. This week memorize Luke 10:27: "Love the LORD your God with all your heart, with all your soul, with all your strength, and with all your mind, and your neighbor as yourself."

Give your heart and your children's hearts to God every morning. Dedicate your day—and then—to Him. Then pray for your precious children as only you, their mom, can!

God, I give You my heart, my day, my children,
and our journeys of faith. I have a renewed
desire to immerse myself in Your Word and to
stand on its truths with commitment and joy.

Your Best Effort

As a mom, God wants you to focus on giving your time and energy to influencing and shaping the hearts of your children toward Him and His purposes.

No matter what your situation at home is, whether your children believe in Jesus or not, whether they're young or older, whether their dad is a Christian or not, or whether he's even in their life at all—or whether or not you've neglected God's Word up until now—do your best.

What you do from this day onward matters greatly. So give it your best effort. If you want your children to love God and follow Him, set the focus of your heart on God, and let them see you love and follow Him.

God, it really does start with me, doesn't it? No matter what else is going on in life, I can choose to follow Your Word and Your leading with a heart of obedience. I want to give my very best efforts to You and to my children.

A Mom Like You

God's not looking for Supermom—He's looking for Godly Mom. Mary was only about 14 when she was chosen to be the human vessel for bringing Jesus into the world. Was she from a wealthy family? An influential family? No. So what qualified her to be blessed and trusted by God? The fabric of her heart. When Mary was told what was about to happen to her, she said, "Behold the maidservant of the Lord! Let it be to me according to your word" (Luke 1:38).

God works through you—a faithful parent, a faithful mom like you who, in spite of dark and difficult days, walks obediently with Him. Ask God to help you pass on your faith and trust in Him so your children might be boys and girls and young men and women who follow Him. And pray, pray…and pray some more!

Jesus, let it be me. Let it be me who walks obediently with You so that faith is etched on my heart and evident in my life. May I lead my little ones to Your embrace.

The Well of Wisdom

When I was a new believer, I was challenged to read one chapter of the book of Proverbs each day. Over the years this has saturated my heart, soul, and mind with God's directions on how to interact with my children, as well as everyone in my life.

Proverbs is a well of wisdom that you can draw from again and again. Journey through Proverbs this year. Give it to yourself as a gift. It will nourish and encourage you. Receive its instruction. Gain God's wisdom. And put it to work in your home. Then pass it on to the next generation. Help your children love and appreciate the book of Proverbs. It will equip them for life!

Thank You, Lord, for Your ever-present, endless supply of help. I will draw from the well of wisdom in Proverbs and let it refresh and saturate my heart and mind. Then let it flow from me to the hearts of my children.

Live It Out

How will being a mom who seeks God's heart and truth be evident in your life and the lives of your children, husband, and friends? Scripture reveals the characteristics you'll begin to adopt, dear mom: Colossians 3:23 says, "Whatever you do, do it heartily, as to the Lord." Be faithful in all things, as it says in 1 Timothy 3:11. Proverbs 31:15 speaks of the woman who "willingly works with her hands." You are also called to do your work with excellence and joy. And you'll learn how to pray without ceasing. And thankfully! First Thessalonians 5:18 says, "In everything give thanks, for this is the will of God in Christ Jesus for you." These are the qualities that show God in your life, mom. Give thanks to God as you live it out day by day.

Father, You show me the beauty of a
life lived with and through faith. I seek
Your heart so that I can know You and
show You to my family and others.

Mother of Nations

You can be a mother of nations! Sound impossible? In Genesis 17:16, God promised Sarah she would be "a mother of nations." And she was—her ancestors included the patriarchs of the faith, kings of nations, and the Savior of the world, Jesus Christ. With Christ in your heart, you begin your own line of godly seed. And your influence goes on and even past your family! How? By speaking up at work, and inviting your friends and neighbors to church. By sharing how Jesus has changed your life, and how He's given you strength and hope. Oh yes—you *can* be a mother of nations!

Lord, I get excited about all the miraculous things You can do when a woman opens up her life to You. I give You the glory today for all that You are doing in me and all that You will do when seeds are planted and faith is shared.

Complex and Demanding

A mother's life is complex *and* demanding. As a woman, you're expected to manage your time wisely, take care of how you look, select and prepare food for the family, coordinate their schedules, discipline and teach the kids, nurture your faith, and inspire your children spiritually. Oh, and be a fantastic wife! Have I left anything out? Are you thinking, *Help! What's a woman to do?*

There's no question life is complicated. My hope and prayer is that you are getting into God's Word and spending time in prayer. Proverbs 2:6 says, "The LORD gives wisdom; from His mouth come knowledge and understanding." As a woman of God, you need every ounce of help and strength you can get. Don't you agree? Live out the busy days of your life—with God's wisdom and His joy!

God, my to-do list feels overwhelming. Give me Your priorities. And give me Your energy. I want to walk through today with renewed hope that in Your strength, I can do all that matters most.

Our Sons and Daughters

Proverbs 31 has parental wisdom worth seeking over and over. Why? Because it is a God-painted portrait of a godly mother teaching her son. Verse 1 reads, "The words of King Lemuel, the utterance which his mother taught him." And just what did she teach him? Morals. Leadership. And fitting behavior for a godly man and future godly leaders. And we see a detailed description of the kind of woman—a godly woman—he was to look for to marry.

Whether you raise a son or a daughter—or both—you're to be a mother who teaches your children the things of the Lord. It takes time, lots of energy, and much perseverance! You already know that. So first things first: Live out God's will in your own life. Then teach it to your sons and daughters!

God, I praise You for the direct, specific example and wisdom You provide in Proverbs 31. The world offers many opinions but very few truths. I need Your Word to walk this road of parenting and to honor this role of a lifetime.

An Added Bonus

If God asked you, like He asked Solomon, "What shall I give you?," what would you answer? Solomon responded by praying, "Lord, give me wisdom." He told God he wanted an understanding heart so he could rightly judge the people. He wanted wisdom so he could discern between good and evil. The Bible says God was pleased with Solomon's request. God gave Solomon what he asked for, and more!

God said, "I have also given you what you have not asked: both riches and honor, so that there shall not be anyone like you among the kings all your days." Isn't it just like our amazing God to add a bonus? God asks you today, "What shall I give you?" What is your heart craving from your Lord? What is your hope for your children?

Lord, when my requests are wise and heartfelt, You multiply my hope and my vision for what could be done. You give beyond my biggest dreams.

Life Can Be Better

Balance. If I only had more balance in my life, things would be soooo much better!" I agree. Balance is a wonderful goal. But it takes more than just wanting it. Discipline in every area of life is crucial. And instead of thinking of it in negative terms, view it as spiritual growth, personal accomplishment, and physical well-being. In other words, a better life.

At times, growth is difficult. Yet you can take comfort in 1 Corinthians 15:57, which says, "Thanks be to God, who gives us the victory through our Lord Jesus Christ." Discipline in your life will be seen by others—and can produce change in them, too. Your kids, friends, neighbors, and coworkers are paying attention. You can be a motivating model and example. Your life can have a positive effect on everyone you live with, know, or encounter!

Jesus, I have victory in Your name. There is not any struggle, goal, or pursuit that is too much for You. Keep me in a praise-and-prayer mode as You do great things in and through me. I'm ready for the beauty of balance.

Dread to Joy

Many women become bored or just plain unhappy in the work they do. If that's the way you feel about your work at home or outside of the home, you can do something about it. You can infuse your life with God's refreshment and His delight. Begin by doing what you do with all your energy. Or as Ecclesiastes 9:10 says, "with all your might" (NIV). Just as if you were doing it for the Lord! And make no mistake—you are. Choose to work with a joyful heart—a servant's heart. You'll find pleasure in what you do if you approach it as a labor of love. Anticipate work with joy instead of dread. And please know I'm fully aware of how dreadful some jobs can be! But God will help you develop a positive attitude toward your work…and your life. Just ask Him!

God, give me a servant's heart in the work I do. When I labor at home or in the workplace, my attitude and diligence reflect my commitment to You. With Your leading I will go from dread to joy.

You Are Set Apart

As a believer in Jesus Christ, you *are* a woman set apart to God. The question to ask is, "Can others tell?" Colossians 3:2 says, "Set your mind on things above, not on things on the earth."

Does your life look like you're set apart to God in what you say and do? What about your attitudes? The way you dress? How you talk to others? Examine the way you treat your friends and family. Every day you are telling others about what matters to you through behaviors, choices, and the things you are involved with. Don't feel pressure to adopt a phony façade. If you're truly a woman after God's own heart, the difference will emerge naturally through your faith priorities. Set your heart on things above!

Father, what do others think of You when they
see my life lived out? I pray that I serve You
well and that I set my heart on things above so
that I am Your faithful child right where I am.

God's Providence

"I just happened to run into Jennifer today. She's going in for surgery next week. I told her we'd be praying." Just happened? I don't think so! God orders even small events to serve the good of His people. Things that may seem accidental to you are directed by God's providence—His design. The truth is God's hand is in all events, including so-called coincidences and chance happenings. If you believe in a sovereign God and His loving providence, choose to consider all that touches your life as God at work. Look for His hand. Believe that He works in all that you encounter and experience, in all that touches your life…and your family! Romans 8:28 reminds us that "all things work together for good to those who love God, to those who are the called according to His purpose."

Lord, I'm eager to experience Your loving sovereignty through special moments and interactions with others. It is exciting to start each day knowing that my life is in the palm of Your hand.

Solitude Is a Requirement

I f you're not spending time with God, the impact of your ministry to people will be shallow at best. It's so easy to think what counts is the time spent in public with people, people, and more people. But the truth is, the greater the proportion of your day spent in quiet, in prayer, in preparation, in meditation—in solitude—the greater your effectiveness. One pastor said to me, "You cannot be with people all of the time and have a ministry to people." I regularly remind myself of a quote that helps me make the right choices: "We must say no not only to things that are wrong, but to things pleasant and good which can hinder our chief work." Your effectiveness for the Lord requires some solitude—roots that grow deep into God!

Jesus, You beckon to me for times of quiet,
times of stillness in Your presence. May
I place my effort and energy toward those
priorities You have placed on my heart.

Spiritual Nutrition

If you've put off your quiet time with God lately, think of regular time in God's Word like you do nutrition—it's absolutely necessary to maintain a healthy life. It's so easy for me to start the day planning to have a devotional time—a little later. Yet a little later never happens! Suddenly I'm off and running. Somehow I failed to set aside the time for the most important relationship in my life.

Can you relate? That's why you have to have habitual, scheduled times with God whether you feel like it or not. You might feel like you don't have the time to spare. But I will share, my fellow mom, that if you feel like that, you need it more than ever. Jesus says that as you draw near to Him, He will draw near to you (James 4:8). What a great promise! Do what you need to do to make it happen, to get the spiritual nutrition you need.

God, my time with You is essential to my spiritual, emotional, and physical wellness. You are the source of all that is good and true. My hunger for wholeness draws me to Your presence.

Write It Down

have godly advice that you won't want to forget. Scribble it on your mirror in lipstick! Write it down and carry it around in your purse! Make it your screensaver! It'll be *that* life changing. Here it is: Make no decision without prayer.

It's a motto I've used with great success to keep me from rushing in and committing myself before I consult God. It guards against the kind of people-pleasing mentioned in Galatians 1:10: "Do I now persuade men, or God?" I rarely have to ask, "How did I get myself into this?" Or "What was I thinking?" As a busy mom, you want to make the wisest decisions possible. I guarantee this spiritual rule will protect your time, family, and purpose.

God, how many times have I faced regrettable
choices? You want to protect me and guide me.
I will come to You with my decisions because
I want to be a follower of Christ in every way.

God-confidence

When you come before the God of the universe, it's easy to wonder if your small needs are worthy of His time. But those doubts usually exist because you doubt your own worth. You can benefit from the tremendous God-confidence that comes from cultivating a heart of prayer. It's much better than self-confidence and self-esteem. God-confidence comes as the Holy Spirit works in you.

As you pray and make choices that honor God, He fills you with His power. When you pray regularly, you experience a divine assurance with every step you take. And that's the kind of God-confidence that will overflow from your life to others. Psalm 100:2 says, "Serve the LORD with gladness." Delight to do His will with the boldness of the Holy Spirit.

Father, You call me to Your presence with
so much love. You view Your children as
precious and worthy. I will come to You
with God-confidence, and I will go about
my role as a mom with that same gift.

Prayer Is a Ministry

When your life centers on diaper changes, the idea of God using you for a ministry sounds crazy, doesn't it? You wonder *How? When?* I know exactly what you'd ask because as a mom with little ones, I faced these questions. But when I came face-to-face with the fact that prayer is a ministry, *everything* changed. I took a notebook and jotted down the names of our church staff, the missionaries we knew, and any requests shared with me. And I joined the church's prayer chain. I joined God in a vital ministry of prayer...and never even had to leave home!

Psalm 34:8 says, "Taste and see that the Lord is good; blessed is the one who trusts in Him!" The blessings that can be yours as you pray are endless. Bow your knees and heart before God and cultivate a heart of prayer. Stand by to watch a *ministry* of prayer unfold.

> *God, I have a place in this world to serve*
> *You through prayer. Show me who needs*
> *my prayers. Transform my heart into that*
> *of a prayer warrior. I am ready, Lord.*

Why This Title?

When I speak to women at conferences, I'm often asked where the inspiration for *A Woman After God's Own Heart* came from. The idea was born when I read about Samuel, who spoke on God's behalf and rebuked Saul for failing to obey God's specific instructions. On several occasions Saul deliberately disobeyed God. He clearly wasn't responsive to God or His laws. After one extreme act of disobedience, God sent Samuel to Saul with this message from 1 Samuel 13:14: "Your kingdom shall not continue. The LORD has sought for Himself a man after His own heart."

God wants a responsive heart, a heart that'll follow His commands and do His will. It's the core of my heart and ministry to call women to be a woman and mom after God's own heart...to call *you* to be that woman.

God, do I seek Your heart? Am I a woman You seek out because I pursue Your heart and truths? I want to be this woman, this mom, this living example of a life that follows You.

Read!

"I used to read my Bible every day. Now I'm not even sure I know where it is!" Oh dear! Find that Bible! Then get yourself a comfy corner, and read. If you're struggling in life, pick up a Bible and read it. If you need help with a relationship, a problem, a decision, then you will find help, comfort, and clarity when you spend time reading God's Word and praying. If you need a renewed passion for God's Word, then set aside some dedicated time every day to discovering it on a personal level. And pray as you read.

Seek the light of God's Word for your life and your family. Commit yourself again to spiritual growth. God says the Bible will not come back to you as void (Isaiah 55:11). It's God's living Word. And it'll make all the difference in every area of your life today and forever.

*Lord, let me dust off my Bible and open
my heart up to all of the living, powerful
influence of Scripture. I long to return to
the confidence and courage Your promises
breathe into my life. Let my children see
me as a mom who loves God's heart.*

Keeping It Straight

God says the key to a life that stays on *His* path is your heart. Simple, right? That is until you get distracted by hardships, wrong priorities, and worries about your children. Then you're in trouble. When God calls you to walk this path of life, you're to look straight ahead. Rather than turning to the right or the left, you're to follow ways that are established by God.

Ask God to write His priorities on your heart and mind. Follow His lead. Ask for help. Seek His path actively. When you do, all the issues, actions, and goings-on of life will be handled His way. A heart responsive to God leads to a life of obedience. And that, dear mom, will help you keep your path straight in line for God's heart.

God, teach me Your priorities. Etch them on my heart. Keep my soul and eyes set on You so that I don't become distracted and discouraged. I want to walk forward and lead my children forward in Your will.

A Most Comparable Helper

A servant spirit? How archaic is that? What I'm looking for is an equal-opportunity marriage!" The problem with this kind of thinking is...well, a problem! Genesis 2:18 says, "It is not good that man should be alone; I will make him a helper comparable to him." A godly mom is a woman with a servant spirit, whether she's married or not. It's her desire to follow in the steps of Jesus, who was the ultimate servant of others, including her family.

When you're married, you're a team and that eliminates any sense of competition between you and your hubby. I became a better Christian and a better wife when I became a better helper. Philippians 2:3 encourages you to be humble and to "esteem others better" than yourself. It's a mind-set that'll help you be more like Christ!

Lord, I want to be a helper and a partner
for my husband. Give me a servant's heart
toward him. Let us work together in this good,
important work of raising godly children.

The Fireplace Story

If you've become a woman who nags, then my fireplace story is a must-read for you! When we decided to do some remodeling in our little house, I was dead-set on a fireplace. I knew we didn't have it budgeted, so I very cleverly made remarks like, "Wouldn't this be the perfect evening for a fire in the fireplace? If we had one!" Or, "Just think, if we had a fireplace, we could have dinner in front of a roaring fire." Finally Jim said, "Elizabeth, are you helping or hindering?" Oops! I vowed to myself never to mention that fireplace again. I made it a matter of prayer so my attitude would change. How about it? Are you willing to give up the nagging? To be a helper instead of a hinderer? Think about what a difference you will make when you stop nagging and you start assisting your husband and your children and praying for them.

God, I confess that I often hinder the health
and wholeness of my family because I am
selfish and stubborn. Release me from
this destructive sin so that I build up
this family you have blessed me with.

Totally Liberating

This might surprise you, but your husband answers to God for leading, and *you* answer to God for following. Ephesians 5:22 says, "Wives, submit to your own husbands, as to the Lord." That means your submission is a choice. You decide whether or not to follow your husband. Do you submit to his leadership as you make decisions about parenting, church involvement, family time? No one can make you do it—not under God's law.

It's an important decision and privilege to defer to follow your husband's leadership. Think of it as your gift! Are you giving the gift of headship? More than that, are you experiencing the rightness that comes from that decision? You will be surprised how liberating it is to submit.

Jesus, I love You, and yet I struggle to submit
to my husband and to Your authority as well.
Let me embrace submission with a committed
heart. Teach me the joy of this freedom. Let
me do it "as to the Lord"—as to You!

A More Powerful Sermon

This special, biblical wisdom is for any wife who has said, "My husband isn't walking with God, so I don't have to listen to his leading." Unless your husband asks you to do something illegal or immoral, God's will is just the opposite. As our kids would say, "Busted!"

First Peter 3:1 presents the following words to help women in this exact situation: "Wives…be submissive to your own husbands, that even if some do not obey the word, they, without a word, may be won by the conduct of their wives." Your submission to your husband preaches a lovelier and more powerful sermon than your mouth ever could. Your conduct counts, and your husband and children are watching the fruit of your faith and heart. Bless them with a message of love.

God, help me follow Your will by following
my husband's leadership. Give me faith
to trust his authority and to always keep
my heart in line with Your own, Lord.

Sheep and Goats

had a very creative teacher when it came to the subject of math. She devised a game called "separating the sheep from the goats." We'd all stand. And each right answer in her math drill meant you could remain standing. In the end, only the "sheep" were standing. The "goats" had been separated out. Diligence is a quality that helps us remain standing as a parent.

Jonathan Edwards said, "Never lose one moment of time, but improve it in the most profitable way possible." I like that! It takes diligence to stay with something until it's finished. It takes action. In Proverbs 31:27 you'll discern a woman who "does not eat the bread of idleness." You become a woman of diligence one day at a time. And diligence practiced today will leave its impact for a lifetime on your children.

God, sometimes I am so tired that I want to quit or give up, even when I know there is parenting work still to be done. Encourage my spirit, Lord. Give me the energy to be a strong, diligent mom.

A Plan that Works

Is your plan for life and faith working? If you answered "No" or "What plan?" then we have work to do! There is a good chance that you are letting bad habits rule your day. It takes 21 days to eliminate a bad habit and replace it with a new one, so we had better get started. Trust me, I've tried the 21-day miracle cure! And I've discovered that it takes much longer to break old habits and create new ones. Why? Because I'm a "repeat offender." Repeat a bad habit often enough and it becomes automatic. Have you fallen into that trap too?

I love Psalm 23:3. It says the Shepherd—the Good Shepherd—"leads me in the paths of righteousness for His name's sake." If you stay close beside Him and walk where He guides you, your habits will honor His name, and you'll display the fruit of the Spirit, the fruit of His righteousness. You'll develop *holy* habits. Now *that's* what I call a plan that *works*!

> *Good Shepherd, I'm excited and determined to shape holy habits as a woman and mom. And when my children and others notice the good changes in my life, I'm giving You all the glory.*

A Better Way

It's great to seek God when we're backed in a corner and we're facing the consequences. But there's a much *better* way to develop a faith life. How about talking to God *before* trouble arrives? Here are some questions I ask myself: What's really important to me? Are these same things important to God? What are my priorities? What *should* they be? Have I given my heart fully to Jesus in all these things? Am I living that commitment? Jeremiah 6:16 says, "Stand in the ways and see, and ask for the old paths, ask where the good way is, and walk in it; then you will find rest for your souls." God will clear the path, the obstacles, and equip you to move forward. He'll show you a better way—His way. You'll enjoy life more and suffer less. Isn't that awesome?

Lord, I spend too much time maneuvering
around obstacles. Today I give my heart
and life to You with renewed zeal. I want
to enjoy these precious days of parenting
and of exploring my purpose in You.

God's Forgiveness Is Complete

I've made serious mistakes in my life. Mistakes that seem unforgivable to me. So how can I expect God to forgive me?" My friend, God's forgiveness is complete. It stretches from Jesus' cross all the way to you!

Give God full control of all of you. Start right now and let Him run your life. He doesn't make mistakes. In fact, He will do a perfect job. If anyone deserved not to be forgiven, it was Paul. Before he met Jesus, Paul incited others to kill and persecute Christians. But it was Paul who was able to say, "Forgetting those things which are behind and reaching forward to those things which are ahead, I press toward the goal for the prize of the upward call of God in Christ Jesus" (Philippians 3:13-14). Isn't that amazing? You can choose to confess and forget the past and press on—in complete and joyful expectation of what God has for you!

God, You forgive me. You love me.
And You allow me to come to You with my
sins and weaknesses so that I can receive Your
grace and strength. Help me extend Your grace
of forgiveness to my children and husband.

A Completely Exposed Heart

How often do people give you a second chance? Not very often, right? And do you hold past mistakes against your kids, spouse, or friends? We might not extend that kind of grace, but God *does*! God's forgiveness is limitless. All you have to do is come to Him with a repentant heart when you sin. Always examine yourself and ask, "Why am I sorry?" Is it for getting caught? Giving in to temptation? Disappointing God? Go to God with a completely exposed heart. He will delight in giving you a thorough and loving cleansing.

You can start the process right now. God can and will give you the grace and strength to do what is necessary to make things right and help you live with any consequences of your actions. With Paul in Philippians 4:13 you can say, "I can do all things through Christ who strengthens me."

Lord, forgive me for my sins today.
I lift up my specific transgressions to You
and You make me clean and whole. Let
mine be a home that is grace-filled.

A Work in Progress

Dear mom, do you ever feel unloved, detached, or disconnected? Do you know and believe that you are a work in progress and will one day be perfect? Philippians 1:6 says to be "confident…He who has begun a good work in you will complete it until the day of Jesus Christ."

If you are feeling "less than" right now or you notice your child experiencing these feelings, remember we are each known and blessed by God. In Jeremiah 1:5 God says, "Before I formed you in the womb I knew you; before you were born I sanctified you." That's pretty special, wouldn't you say? And in Romans 5:8 Paul reminds us that "God demonstrates His own love toward us, in that while we were still sinners, Christ died for us." We're complete in Christ. Share this message with your family and live your life supporting them as works in progress.

Lord, I can be hard on myself and I see my family
doing the same sometimes. We are deeply loved
by You, our Savior. Work in us. Help us live
in the confidence and peace of our salvation.

It Keeps Me Together

Finding a way to experience God's peace is essential when you are a mom. In my case, it is the quiet time in the morning with my Bible and notebook that keeps me together. When I don't meet with the Lord regularly, it's easy to forget the power and assurance that time with Him brings. A daily time in God's Word and in prayer will renew your calmness and strength—to say nothing about your perspective!

When you meet a stressful situation, look to the Lord. Draw on His composure and peace. As Psalm 46:10 says, "Be still, and know that I am God." As you well know, that can be the only place you'll find stillness! Show your children how to seek the peace of God's presence while they are young. This will serve them, and the Lord, well.

Father, forgive me for not coming to You sooner.
I overload my schedule, work late hours, and
treat quiet time as though it is idle time. I'm on
my way back to Your peace-giving presence, Lord!

The Prayer Spotlight

When a woman shares that her husband drives her nuts, other women quickly nod in understanding. And if this is you, you're not alone, my friend. But I've discovered it's almost impossible to neglect, hate, or even be driven crazy by a person you're praying for, including your husband! And your kids.

Before you give up on that good man you married, invest your time and heart in praying for him. One day you'll wake up and find the arguments are less, and there's a mellowing, even a warming, in your heart toward him. You'll realize that while you were praying for your husband, God changed you and your heart. Jesus said in Matthew 6:21, "Where your treasure is [in this case, the treasure of your time and effort in prayer], there your heart will be also." Treasure your husband today.

God, I lift up my husband to You today.
Infuse him with courage and encouragement
to be a good parent, partner, and man
of God. Give me a great, sincere heart
for the man You and I both love.

Build and Build and Build

I hear that all too often! Proverbs 14:1 begins, "The wise woman builds her house," and it ends, "But the foolish pulls it down." For instance, what does anger out of control do? It throws, it slams, it tears, and it rips. And it speaks words that break and destroy and ruin. The wise woman of this verse knows that she's on assignment from God, that building a home is a lifelong project. Wisdom—*God's* wisdom in His Word—builds and builds and builds.

As it is with most things, the attitude of your heart is key. In fact, it's vital! Decide right now to identify and stop destructive habits that are pulling down and destroying what you're trying to build for your children. And instead, build to the glory of God!

Jesus, You build and create and transform.
I often let my frustrations take over good
intentions. That's why I need Your help
and wisdom. Give me firm conviction over
the bad habits I need to be done with.

Make Your Bed

❧

Do you battle your children every day over the importance of them making their beds? It seems the national media agrees with you. I read an article that listed the top ten reasons to adopt this habit. The number one reason might surprise you! It is because the bed is the biggest object in the room. So it is logical that if you make your bed, you improve 80 percent of the room with one simple action. Anything I can do easily for that kind of return is wonderful in my book! But no efficiency takes the place of your heart attitude. Search your heart and your home. Where are you placing your focus and investing your energy? Proverbs 31:27 says, "She watches over the ways of her household." Is that you? Take God's wisdom and ways to heart. That's what being a smart mom after God's own heart is all about!

Father, show me all of Your ways. Let me absorb Your wisdom, apply it, and pass it along to my children on a regular basis. The return for this invested time and commitment is eternal!

Love Works

You come home tired, or you're tired after a full day of working at home and coordinating the kids' lives. So why is the chore of fixing dinner always on *your* plate? That's a good and fair question! But my answer may surprise you: You're driving into the driveway and behind you, your husband's pulling up. Both of you have put in a long, hard day. So who *is* fixing dinner? Or washing the dishes? Or making lunches? *Someone* has to do all of these tasks. I like what Edith Schaeffer said: "To whom can you demonstrate love in the day-by-day, mundane circumstances of life?" Not only that, you're to do good, expecting nothing in return. Wow. That takes a little thinking about, doesn't it? In John 15:12 Jesus said, "This is my commandment, that you love one another as I have loved you." Go for it—give it a try and let me know if love works for you!

Lord, my husband is sometimes the last person
I extend myself and my service for. Help me
to love him in my heart and through my
actions. He is my life partner and my partner
in parenting. Is there anyone more important?

A Heart of Kindness

Being good and being kind all the time and to everyone can be downright tiring. The secret to not becoming jaded, burned out, or inauthentic is to adapt your attitude to God's. Will you get it right every time? No, not unless you're the perfect woman, and I have yet to meet her! But if you want to exhibit the character of God in your life and you're willing to make some choices to make it happen, you're right on track.

Keep focused on God's plan for you in His Word—one day at a time. The Bible says you're to put on a heart of kindness, compassion, and goodness. Make it your daily habit to be a woman of the Word of God. Pray. Ask for God's help, for His grace. Then follow through—faithfully!

God, I want to show others Your great kindness and compassion. I purpose to seek Your heart and learn from Your Word and Your loving nature. I want to pursue good and godly attitudes. Open my heart up wide, Lord!

Make It Your Resolve

What is it about resolutions that fill us with delightful anticipation…and dread? At first we are hopeful. But unfortunately we begin to doubt our ability to keep a resolution. Embrace this list of godly resolutions so that you have the strength of the Lord leading the way: (1) Never worry about your self-worth, but instead, (2) rejoice in your worth to God. Psalm 139:14 says you are "fearfully and wonderfully made." (3) Determine you're going to seek a deeper relationship with God, and (4) you're going to walk by faith even when you don't always understand God's direction.

How much time are you spending each day in God's Word? How much time in prayer? It's not a matter of legalism, but of relishing what you have in Christ! Doing these things will give you strength and hope each day to follow through with your resolve to reflect God's glory in your life.

> *Lord, give me the hope and faith of godly*
> *resolutions. With Your leading, I can*
> *accomplish anything, including being*
> *a mom after Your own heart.*

What's It Worth?

I love John Wesley's words, "My gift is speaking my mind. God has told me I don't have to exercise that gift." Our behavior reflects our heart. So you have to ask yourself: Do I love other people by being careful with what I say? Am I in control of my passions? Am I willing to serve others? Am I loving with a sacrificial love?

When you consider the remarkable gifts of love and forgiveness that God has given to you through Jesus, is it too much for Him to ask your obedience? The Bible says, "God is love" (1 John 4:8). He *is* love. May you as a woman and a mom continue to grow and love Him and others even more.

> *Lord, I love my children and yet I see how*
> *their attitudes can be trouble. Am I the*
> *same way sometimes? Help me grow into a*
> *loving woman who honors You. Thank You*
> *for this gift of love You have given to me.*

Enough Time

❦

How are you doing? Are you merely surviving? Just getting by? Or are you able to find a way to live a faithful and fulfilled life? One mom told me, "I'm really having difficulty managing being a mother, wife, and employee. I spend weekends trying to catch up but I feel like I'm drowning." Many women feel this pressure.

It may seem impossible, but spend time every day thinking and praying about today and tomorrow—even a week out. It'll help you manage your priorities, and even give you a few minutes to spend in prayer or reading your Bible. I know it won't be easy—but it's not impossible! Philippians 4:13 says, "I can do all things through Christ who strengthens me." That's great news for a busy mom. Bless you for all you do—and *are*!

Jesus, please give me discernment and Your
perspective as I prioritize and manage my day
today and my week ahead. Help me do my best
for my family by devoting time to spend with You.

Time Wasters

In real estate, it's all about location, location, location. In life, it's prioritize times three! What can you remove from your life that's not a priority? It takes discipline, but the reward is great. Eliminate whatever doesn't contribute positively to God's plan for your life. Look for the "stuff" that isn't essential and adds to our burden of busyness. Then make the call. Is it going to be in...or out? You might discover that you really enjoy this process.

Ephesians 5:15-16 says, "Walk circumspectly, not as fools but as wise, redeeming the time." Spending an hour on the Internet or Facebook isn't a bad thing. But you can choose to eliminate that if it's impacting what's most important. Every day ask, "How can I better live this day?"

God, what needs to go? What priority am
I neglecting? How can I better live this day?
How can I honor this life You've given to me
and enjoy the blessings of family and faith?

Making Time Count

Evaluate your day. Note what you did that wasted time—too much TV, too much texting, too much negotiating bath and bedtime with your kids? The Bible just happens to have a checklist that will help you with your faith commitments and prayer life. Take a look at Titus 2:3-5: "Teach the older women to be reverent in the way they live, not to be slanderers or addicted to much wine, but to teach what is good. Then they can urge the younger women to love their husbands and children, to be self-controlled and pure, to be busy at home, to be kind, and to be subject to their husbands" (NIV).

Make these "essentials" your priorities. Plan them into your days with intention and deliberation. You'll be amazed at your use of time. And it'll make a huge difference in what you focus on and how you spend your days.

Lord, thank You for the inspiration of Your life
essentials. I need this boost of hope and energy.
Help me remember to wake up each morning
excited to practice the art of godly living!

Consider It All Joy

Susannah Spurgeon was the wife of preacher Charles Spurgeon. She suffered from physical problems that grew worse over time. She said: "When the fire of affliction draws songs of praise from us, then indeed our God is glorified." And amazingly she added, "Let the furnace be heated seven times hotter than before!" To her, it became joy in the fire. Joy through tears and pain.

Hannah was Susannah's biblical counterpart. In 1 Samuel 2:2 she prays: "No one is holy like the LORD... nor is there any rock like our God." Hannah suffered terribly in her life. But despite the suffering, she knew God understood her difficulties. For her, too, joy would come from God, and God alone. James 1:2 says, "Count it all joy when you fall into various trials." He will see you through!

Lord, so many women of God have blazed trails of hope and faith because of their trials. Let me be one of these women who possesses joy because they depend on Your strength and guidance.

You Are What You Think

Proverbs 23:7 says you are the result of what you're thinking in your heart. That can be scary! When I was a new Christian, my thoughts didn't always turn heavenward. It's still a goal that requires my willful decision every day. Philippians 4:8 says to think upon whatever is true, noble, just, pure, lovely, good, virtuous, and praiseworthy. Make the decision each day to willfully think about God, think through passages of Scripture. You'll be amazed at what this does for your life, to say nothing about your thoughts.

Also, gather more spiritual strength by memorizing Scripture. There's nothing like God's words in your heart to turn your thoughts toward Him. David prayed, "Let the words of my mouth and the meditation of my heart be acceptable in your sight, O Lord." Make that *your* prayer as well!

> *God, You know what's in my heart and*
> *mind and You know what needs to*
> *change. Help me to cultivate a heart that*
> *reflects You, Your love, truth, and virtue.*

Renewing Your Mind

Time spent curled up with a good book—what's not to like about that? Let me just make a suggestion. Fiction is great entertainment. But if you want to grow spiritually, some of that reading time has to be spent in God's Word. That's what will allow you to view life and circumstances through a lens of truth. When you read God's Word, you tune in to God's heart and His teaching.

Romans 12:2 says the Word of God renews your mind. It transforms your thoughts. So let me ask you this: Is what you're thinking today, even right now, a reflection of the media you're immersed in, or is it the fruit of God's Word? There's nothing—*nothing* that can renew your mind like God's Word!

Lord, when I get discouraged and overwhelmed,
I need to turn from the world's voice and
enter the solace of Your teachings and truth.
Alone with You, my mind will be renewed.

A Spiritual Gift

How exciting to think of serving God in big and small ways! You're not only commanded to give your life in service, but you're gifted and equipped by God to serve. I find that truly amazing and hopeful. Your service will glorify God. It takes on a supernatural quality because it's not you—it's not natural. And it's not explainable. Your service involves using a spiritual gift, ministered by the power of the Holy Spirit working in and through you. First Peter 4:10 says, "As each one has received a gift, minister it to one another, as good stewards of the manifold grace of God." What amazing grace!

Your willingness to follow God's direction in your life will become an example to your children as they discover their own gifting.

God, reveal to me my gifts and abilities. When I am afraid to move forward in service, let me depend on the strength of the Holy Spirit to step beyond fear to an abundant life of ministry.

Ask for Wisdom

Like you, I can easily get bombarded with all kinds of demands—as a woman, a wife, and a mom! That's when I need help with being wise. Wise in living. Wise in knowing what to do. Remember the genie in the bottle—ask anything you want and it'll be granted? Well God appeared to Solomon in a dream and said, "What shall I give you?" And Solomon answered, "Wisdom and discernment."

God gave Solomon his wish—a heart that was wise and understanding. Wisdom is the ability to view life as God perceives it. That's what you should want too! And the best part? It's yours to desire above all else. Dear sister and special mom, *pray* for wisdom and ask for what you need from the good Lord.

Lord, I'm too slow in asking for help. But
I need Your wisdom. I want to lead my
children in noble, godly practices. You have
entrusted me with their training and my own
life decisions. Help me to ask for Your help.

What a Woman!

I want you to meet a woman I highly admire and respect. There's so much to learn from her—her name is Abigail. Do yourself a huge favor and take the time today to read her story in 1 Samuel 25. She was a woman who knew about stress, about being married to an alcoholic and a tyrant. What a tightrope Abigail walked...yet she was so wise and righteous. Her life was characterized by wise actions, wise speech. She dazzled everyone when she used that God-given wisdom to squelch a battle between her foolish husband and David and his 400 troops. She knew what to do and when to do it. Every challenge or responsibility you have can be handled with this same godly wisdom. Do you believe it? Do you trust God as you face troubles in your marriage and as you raise your children? Let *your* life be characterized by wisdom!

> *Lord, when I think I have my act together,*
> *everything falls apart. I'm trusting only*
> *my opinion and faulty logic rather than*
> *true wisdom. I want to be a woman who*
> *shines with authenticity, integrity, and*
> *a deep understanding of Your truths.*

Ask of God

James 1:5 says if you lack wisdom, you can ask of God. And here's the best part—it *will* be given to you! Here's what I suggest you do *today*. Just as soon as you can. Read a chapter from the book of Proverbs; the chapter that corresponds with the day of the month. Do this every day, and each time, pick one verse that speaks to your heart and life. Write it down. Carry it with you all day. Put it out where you can see it on your desk, your table, wherever you are—have that card with you. Proverbs 9:10 says, "The fear of the LORD is the beginning of wisdom, and the knowledge of the Holy One is understanding." Open your heart, and bow before the Lord today.

God, uh-oh...I lack wisdom. It's true.
I'm barely getting by as I try to parent, work,
survive, juggle, and stay on top of burdens
like debt and loneliness. You want me
to live a transformed life. Give me Your
wisdom and hope, Lord. I need it so.

Love One Another

There's a proverb that says, "A whisperer separates the best of friends" (16:28). There's a popular cable TV show about women who *talk* about each other. That's entertainment? Bottom line: Gossip is harmful! How much is gossip a part of your interactions with friends or your children?

As one of God's women, you are called to be a helper, a teacher, and encourager of women. That leaves no room for gossip. Your entire ministry of encouragement shuts down when you speak words that wound. And those words can never be taken back. Oh that we would be like Jesus, who "committed no sin, nor was deceit found in his mouth" (1 Peter 2:22). God asks you to serve and better the lives of others—including your family and friends—and no life has ever been uplifted by gossip. Instead, do as Jesus commands you: Love one another.

Lord, I am humbled today. I know that my speech is not without sin. I do use sarcasm and negative talk in front of my children and toward other women. Keep my speech limited to words that build up and do not tear down. Forgive me.

The Prodigal Returns

have so many used-to's in my life. I used to read the Bible regularly. I used to be more connected in my church. I used to pray more openly." So how do we get off track? How does a prodigal become a prodigal? You *know* what happens, don't you? You get busy with other things and God's Word takes a secondary place. Soon your passion for God is burned out and you feel lost. But God has given you a map for your life in His Word. It teaches you, corrects you, mends you, instructs you, equips you, and cheers you along the way. What more could you want?

Do whatever it takes to get that passion back. Return to the Lord today. Start today to get back into God's Word—even if it's just minutes. You've been there, you know what it takes. And you know what it's worth in your life!

God, restore to me the joy and wonder of diving into Your Word and instruction. Let me read it as Your personal love letter, as the treasury of wisdom and map for living that it is!

You Have What It Takes

It's easy to let your busyness ease the pain of an empty marriage. How about it? Sound familiar? Hobbies, kids' activities, classes, workouts, volunteer projects, friends, shopping…anything to avoid being at home. But let me tell you—these other things will never take the place of a happy marriage. Why not put the same time, effort, and energy into making your marriage what God intended it to be? You have what it takes because you have God and His power in your life. And 2 Corinthians 12:9 promises His grace! Whatever you do, don't allow the culture around you to cloud God's view of the importance of your marriage. God means for your marriage to be filled with passion and purpose. And it can be!

God, don't let me use my activities or the kids to avoid dealing with the needs or issues of my marriage. Encourage me in the work of building a lasting relationship with my hubby. In Your strength, I can nurture my marriage.

Learn to Be Content

Contentment is not based on circumstances. The apostle Paul knew that. He wrote that he *learned* to be content. It doesn't come automatically. That should encourage you. And contentment is vital even when you have more than enough. That's because having much breeds wanting even more. John Wesley said, "When I have any money I get rid of it as quickly as possible, lest it find a way into my heart." We say to ourselves, "If the kids would mind better, I'd be content." It just isn't true.

You already have all the true riches of heaven. You have the hope of eternal life, no matter what's going on right now. John 16:33 says you "will have tribulation." But you also have Christ. That means you can have contentment of soul *in the midst* of our circumstances, including those that are difficult or uncertain.

*Lord, I let how things are going with the kids
or my husband, or the ups and downs of my
mood, dictate my sense of contentment. Release
me from this false living so that I truly know
the security and joy of contentment in You.*

God Will Meet Real Needs

"We owe so much! It's like a black cloud over our heads—and over our family." This reflects the heart cries of many moms today, maybe even you. Being in debt is a form of bondage. It stifles your freedom to enjoy life, and it prevents you from helping others. Go on a spending fast! No frivolous purchases you don't need. Our family has done that several times over the years. It gives you a renewed appreciation for personal discipline and all that God faithfully provides.

Here's a caution: Don't spend more than you make. And realize that buying on credit gives you a false sense of security. God is glorified when you wait on Him to provide for you. Mom, that's a life-changing truth. Pray for the patience to wait. Let God meet your real needs. He will—in His ways and in His timing.

Lord, it is so hard to live within our means
right now. We are struggling, and yet I know
You are caring for us. Forgive my lack of trust
and vision. I will depend on Your provision
so You are glorified and my heart is free.

A Cheerful Giver

Do you have a generous spirit? God *loves* a cheerful giver! I can remember the day I began praying on my daily walk. My first prayer request was to become more generous. I had examined my heart and found myself way lacking in this area! So I began praying about it daily, asking God for awareness of opportunities to give and ways to serve the needs of others, including my own family. As the apostle Paul said, "Let each one give as he purposes in his heart." *Purpose* to give…and you'll receive God's blessings. Proverbs 31:20 says of the woman described there, "She extends her hand to the poor, yes, she reaches out her hands to the needy." Her hands were open. She literally—and cheerfully—"rushed" to give. We should be so faithful.

Jesus, in what areas is my heart lacking?
What do I need to do to live out my faith?
Show me how my gifting, my experience,
and my belief can make a difference.

Best Friends

After you get married, it can be difficult to carve out time for friends or to make your husband a priority if you are more drawn to girlfriend time. Of *course* friends are important—for encouragement, sharing, and companionship. But your husband is first priority! You're to love your husband as your *best* friend—as a cherished, intimate mate.

In Song of Solomon 5:16 a man says of his bride, "This is my beloved, and this is my friend." What would the words to *your* song say? If that's not true of your heart and your marriage, and that special friend relationship has been eroded, ask God to work in your heart. You and your husband were best friends at one time—it can be true again! That's great news!

*Lord, help me to want to be my husband's
companion and friend. Give us times to
just be together without talking about
the kids or the bills. I miss him, Lord.*

The In-law Factor

Let's talk about your relationship with your parents and in-laws. The Bible is full of teachings about the respect and honor parents are due. Ephesians 6:2 says, "Honor your father and mother, which is the first commandment with promise; that it may be well with you and you may live long on the earth." It's not optional—it's a command!

There are no excuses. As a Christian woman, you are to honor your parents, and you are to show this same respect to your in-laws. You reveal the level of your spiritual maturity in these important relationships. God has given you all the grace and all the character resources you need to get along with anyone—including your parents and in-laws. And never forget that you're modeling to your children how they should treat you and their future relatives.

> *Father, give me a heart for my parents and my husband's parents. Help me work on deepening our relationships. Encourage me to lead my children to nurture these important connections to family and to their heritage—in life and in faith!*

A Faithful Friend

There's an English proverb that says, "God save me from my friends; I can take care of my enemies." I've been burned by some who I thought were my friends. And I'm guessing you have too. As hurtful as it is, the most important thing in your friendships is that *you* be loyal. You cannot be responsible for other people's behavior, but you *are* responsible for yours.

Teach your children about loyalty and faithfulness through friendships. At any age, they may experience the hardship of losing a friend. Proverbs 27:10 says, "Do not forsake your own friend." A true friend stands by no matter what—even when a painful truth must be told: "Faithful are the wounds of a friend" (27:6). My advice? Stay true. Stay faithful. And when it's best to do so, stay quiet.

Jesus, You are my example of faithfulness and kindness. Don't let me get caught up in blame or petty disputes. Give me a bottomless love for those I call friend. Help me love others the way You love me.

Love Isn't a Scorekeeper

Some women are great at forgetting...but not forgiving. Others have the forgiveness part down (so they say), but then dwell on a past wrongdoing. If you take any approach other than forgiving *and* forgetting, you're missing out on much of what Jesus said about friendship! I remember reading in 1 Corinthians 13 that love thinks no evil, and I thought I knew what it meant. But there's a lot more to it. It means love doesn't keep score. True friends and godly parents don't keep a list of wrongs or failures or offenses. You don't say to your child or your neighbor, "I'll give you one chance at this—and that's it!" Proverbs 17:17 says, "A friend loves at all times." It's unconditional.

God, help me to not hold grudges and keep
track of wrongdoings committed by friends
or family. This is no way to live. Give me
grace and a heart of love—of friendship!

It's About Distractions

A woman's dream house has a room for each child *and* a room big enough for all her shoes! Okay, I'm laughing and I think I hear you doing the same. But it's amazing how distracted you can get over the most unimportant things. The truth is, there's so much more to think about, to do, and to be! It's not the shoes that are the problem. It's the preoccupation with *anything* that keeps you from being all God wants you to be. That includes what you dream about and think about.

Philippians 4:8 should inspire you to think on those things that are noble. Pure. Lovely. Praiseworthy. You're to treasure in your heart thoughts that are rich and uplifting. God calls you—He *commands* you—to think heavenly, godly thoughts. Are your thoughts worthy to bring into God's presence? Think on it.

*God, You know my thoughts...and the
distractions that keep me from godly focus
and pursuits. Make the product of my
heart and mind worthy of Your presence.*

Busy All the Time

Decisions, decisions. It seems that every second moms must make decisions for themselves or their children. We're busy! But I challenge you to not give away all your precious time to whims of the moment. Schedule your day to include time with God. Organize your life according to God's priorities. Schedule your day so that God is glorified and the people in your life are blessed.

I love the words from the heart of David Brainerd, a missionary, a man who lived his life with passion and purpose. "Oh how precious is time; and how guilty it makes me feel when I think I have trifled away and misimproved it or neglected to fill up each part of it with duty to the utmost of my ability and capacity." Are you filling up time with what matters?

*Lord, lead me to bless my husband, kids,
friends, neighbors, and others I should serve.
Give me a clear sense of how to use each
moment so that I am a blessing to others.*

Stay Focused

Do you, dear mom, awaken with good intentions and then watch them fade away as the day unfolds? Your focus for the day will be transformed if you *begin* it with the Lord. The act of using your mind to read your Bible changes your thinking, perspective, choices, behavior, and the way you live your life.

You never know how or when God will use you and your unique gifts. But if you prepare spiritually, there will always be opportunities. Your job is to prepare and then look to God. His job is to determine when you're ready. And that will happen in His timing! Ephesians 2:10 says, "We are His workmanship, created in Christ Jesus for good works." He wants to use you. The best you have to offer is a lot—it is God's best. So stay focused!

Father, my intentions and my good and noble thoughts fall away as soon as the baby cries or a new life stress emerges. I will begin my day with You so that all I do reflects Your very best.

Don't Waste Your Mind

🌹

It took Michelangelo four years to paint the ceiling of the Sistine Chapel. He had to paint with his head tilted uncomfortably upward while standing on scaffolds held by brackets in the walls, some 60 feet above the floor. Amazing! He never stopped using his mind, his creativity, his energy. And neither should you! You can grow and be creative.

Once you have children, you focus so much on their development that it's easy to forget to nurture yourself. You can pray, read the Bible, memorize Scripture, use your gifts. Develop your mind and heart by focusing on God. Commit yourself to the things that lead to living a godly life. Guard your heart, and don't waste your mind—or your life. They are too precious to be spent on anything that doesn't help you live out God's plan and purposes for your life.

This life is precious, Lord. I believe that. I watch days pass by and I feel like I'm missing out. Don't let me waste another minute. Let me grow in spiritual strength, creativity, knowledge, and in all ways that serve my family and Your purposes.

Don't Wait—Serve

I f you're waiting to discover your gifts and talents—*don't*! There are so many things we're commanded to do. It doesn't take a lightning bolt from God to know these commands are for *you*. First Peter 1:22 says to love one another fervently. Serving, giving, and showing mercy—each day live out these commands. A great example for women is found in Luke 8:2-3, where we're told of a group of faithful women who used their money and resources to help support Jesus and His disciples on their preaching tours. You can accomplish great things when you act in God's will. Don't wait. Start serving your husband, kids, community, and Lord.

Jesus, You were served by godly women when You walked the earth. What a special joy it is to know that I don't have to wait for more experience, more education, more money. You call me to service right here, right now.

A Contented Woman

Would people say you're a contented woman? Satis-fied with what you have? I want you to meet some-one—I wish I knew her name. The Bible only refers to her as the "Shunammite woman" in 2 Kings 4. What a picture of contentment she is for you today. She was a caring, generous person God used to provide room and board for His prophet Elisha. When Elisha asked what he could give to repay her many kindnesses, she said, "Nothing! What more could I possibly want or need?" She understood grace, contentment, and service. May you too extend kindness to others without expecting anything in return. May you delight in what you already have. May you look at your children with cereal milk on their lips and at your house that's a bit too small and say, "What more could I possibly need or want?"

Father, I have so many blessings right now,
and still I tend to focus on what's missing.
I love this Shunammite woman and want
to become like her, a woman who finds
peace, plenty, and joy in her chance to serve.

Let the Stretching Begin

Many moms feel the stress of time always being in short supply. The good news is that the real issue is not our time allotment, but how we manage our time. Time management is very freeing when you look at it as a means to growth, ministry, and doing what God calls you to do. The body of Christ needs your gifts and what only you have to offer. If you manage your life with passion and purpose, you *will* have time to serve, support, and teach others.

When opportunities for ministry come your way, opportunities that promise to stretch you, be ready. This starts with making sure you are growing. Then be prepared. Be a good manager of time and energy. Look to the Lord for your help, then let the stretching begin!

God, I am truly willing to stretch and grow.
Help me to stretch my time by managing it
as a good steward and a godly woman.

A Heart of Love

feel pulled in too many directions. It's not a lack of love on my part. I'm just tired." I understand where this mom is coming from. When I'm stressed, the *last* thing I want to do is reach out again. When you feel the least able to love, you are still able to serve with a deliberate act of your will. You can, with God's grace, give love when you want to withhold it, reach out to others when you want to rest, and serve when you'd rather be served.

Ephesians 5:2 guides you to "walk in love, as Christ also has loved us and given Himself for us." When you're frustrated and worn out, look to God for His love, He will give you a God attitude—a *heart* of love!

Jesus, when I follow You, I can walk in love.
Your grace provides me with the strength and
motivation I need to serve and reach out. I want
my life to be infused with Your heart of love.

Love—a Sacrifice of Self

It's easy to love people who love in return. But what about those who don't? Jesus makes this astounding statement in Matthew 5:44-45: "I say to you, love your enemies, bless those who curse you, do good to those who hate you…that you may be sons of your Father in heaven." God *expects* you to love the unloving, just as He loved you when you were lost in sin. God's love is *never* deserved—it simply *is*.

It's natural for you to expect that when you're nice to others, they'll return the kindness, right? Wrong! And you probably have the scars to prove it. Yet Jesus said, without exception, "Love one another; as I have loved you, that you also love one another" (John 13:34). Love is the sacrifice of self for the sake of your husband, your children, and even your enemies.

Lord, it is hard to care about those who
don't care in return. But I will look at
each of these people through Your eyes
of love—Your unconditional love.

The Right Thing at the Right Time

I can't tell you the number of times I've meant to say the right thing—and didn't! It's too easy to have negative thoughts even toward your cherished family and friends. And then when you do have an opportunity to offer words of encouragement, your negative heart takes over, and you miss your chance to do the right thing. The loving thing. To overcome that, you need to apply biblical guidelines to the ways you think and talk.

Philippians 4:8 says to meditate on "whatever things are true, whatever things are noble, whatever things are just, whatever things are pure, whatever things are lovely, whatever things are of good report." When you do, your response changes. Nurture a heart of love—and use your tongue to glorify God.

God, I will think on what is good and
righteous so that when You give me a
chance to encourage, to be there for another,
I am ready, willing, and fully able!

Sparkle

Many women say they want to "be happy." The problem with pursuing happiness is that it depends on the circumstances around you in life—which can change as often, and as quickly, as the weather!

The reason a jeweler will show a diamond against a black cloth is so that when light hits all its facets, the sparkle contrasts more brightly against the dark backdrop. Joy is like this—it is the brightest when set against the darkness of trials and testing. Joy in the Lord has nothing to do with your situation. Rather, it comes from within and has everything to do with your relationship to Jesus. Your joy is rooted in an unchanging, totally faithful God. It's permanent. You can take His joy *wherever* you go, no matter what happens in life!

> *Thanks to You, Lord, I have joy that*
> *goes with me wherever I go. It is my*
> *experience, no matter what is happening*
> *to me. And it leads me to shine against the*
> *background of my darkest hardship.*

God Is Sufficient

Ah, peace! How would you define it? As a lack of problems? A sense that all is well? Peace isn't related to circumstances. Not God's peace. His peace endures—regardless! It has nothing to do with life situations. Nothing to do with any crisis you might face today. It has everything to do with knowing that whatever happens is in God's hands. Knowing that God is all-sufficient in every situation. David was able to say in Psalm 139:8-10, "If I ascend into heaven, You are there; if I make my bed in hell, behold, You are there. If I... dwell in the uttermost parts of the sea, even there, Your hand shall lead me." Peace isn't the absence of conflict; it's the *presence* of God—no matter what the conflict. *Rest* in that thought!

> *God, I have always waited for peace to come*
> *when chaos clears and all my problems are*
> *solved. Give me wisdom and insight about*
> *what Your peace feels like, looks like, and*
> *can accomplish when I walk in it.*

The Gold Standard

The world we live in holds up money as the standard for success. But one of the best lessons you can teach your children isn't about investing in the right markets, but investing in their name—their character. Proverbs 22:1 says, "A good name is to be chosen rather than great riches." Your character and that of your children is more important than money. Your reputation is more valuable than wealth. It says in Proverbs 16:16, "How much better to get wisdom than gold! And to get understanding is to be chosen rather than silver." Teach your children godly behaviors and attitudes, and they will increase the value of their reputation. And their hearts will be invested in God's great abundance of contentment, joy, and purpose. A good reputation and a life of honor is better than gold!

*Lord, help me to raise up my children to respect
and honor their reputation. Let their actions
and words bring glory to You and Your name.*

Answered Prayer

Does it ever seem as if God isn't answering your prayers? Actually, God *does* answer prayer. Matthew 7:7 says, "Ask, and it will be given you; seek, and you will find; knock, and it will be opened to you." As you grow in your understanding of God's powerful promise of answered prayer, keep in mind you need to make sure your requests are in faith. That is, as James 4:3 says, we're to pray without selfish motives and according to the will of God. Sometimes you don't get answers because you don't ask. You worry, you talk to others, but you don't bring the matter to the Lord. And when you think your prayers aren't being answered, you blame God. But Jesus said, "Ask, and you will receive" (John 16:24). Isn't that great news?

> *God, I've been fretting a lot, but I haven't come to You to seek Your guidance and make my requests known. Thank You for hearing the needs of my heart today.*

A Heart Transplant

guess I'm happy. I just thought my life would somehow be…well, more!" It's easy to think this way after a hard day of parenting. This feeling is an opportunity to make a change—a change of heart. In the Old Testament God promised to give His people "a new heart…a new spirit… [and] take the heart of stone out" (Ezekiel 36:27). God's promise of change says that when we are in Christ, we become new creatures. "Old things have passed away; behold, all things have become new" (2 Corinthians 5:17)! John 3 calls this a new birth. God gives you a spiritual heart transplant! He replaces that heart of stone with a heart of flesh. And this new heart works in, out, and through your life—and your marriage and family. It brings change. What a difference that makes! It's not just being happy, it's joy. It's…well, it's more!

Lord, You give me a daily opportunity to
make my life into something more, by giving
it over to You and Your guidance. You will
create that special something out of this
everyday living. I praise You for that.

Reach Out and Touch

There are many moms who deal with loneliness. Are you a single mom? Or are you feeling disconnected from your husband? Is he deployed or required to travel on the job? We all need a shoulder to cry on after a hard day. And what day of parenting isn't a bit hard? Whatever's going on with you that triggers the aloneness—God is there to help and to comfort you. Psalm 147:3 is just one of many promises that reminds you He is an all-powerful God who chooses to reach down and heal the brokenhearted. It's a promise! Rest in it.

Be encouraged. Your suffering and God's comfort become your teachers so that you can, in turn, reach out and give comfort and strength to others. Won't you lead others to the shoulder and heart of God? Reach out and touch someone—including your kids and their dad—today.

God, I come to You today for comfort.
Reassurance. Cover me in Your love and
give me Your peace. I will tell of Your
goodness and share of Your lasting comfort.

Signposts

Are you looking for direction? Would a few sign-posts help? As you discover and grow in the use of your primary spiritual gifts, use this little checklist to receive assurances: Is what you're doing bringing you joy? That's a strong indicator of giftedness. Your service should cause others to be blessed. So what does God seem to be blessing most? Your service will be affirmed by others. What are people thanking you for? And your service will create opportunities to serve more! What are you being asked to do?

A ministry done unselfishly and unreservedly in the Spirit will glorify not you, but God. Serving the Lord will lead you to more signposts and more opportunities to serve. God is so good!

Father, I desire to follow the signposts of Your guidance. I love my family and want to live as an example of one who pursues her heavenly Father's heart and direction without hesitation…and with praises on my lips.

God Is Not Finished with You

Does it seem that you take three steps forward and two steps back in your walk with Christ? Be encouraged. When God starts a project—that's you—He completes it. When you feel unfinished, incomplete, or like a failure, God is at work in you. When you doubt your parenting skills or how to make your way in the world, God is still at work in you.

Paul says in Philippians 1:6, "Being confident of this very thing, that He who has begun a good work in you will complete it until the day of Jesus Christ." Paul wrote this because his friends were maturing in their Christian faith, and he wanted to share his confidence that God would be faithful to continue the spiritual growth He began in their lives. God will do the same for you and me.

Lord, I get excited when I think about
the finishing work You are doing in my
life—both as a mom and a woman of God.
Give me the confidence and courage that
comes from knowing You will lead me.

Confident and Sure

I f I could, I'd make it possible for every woman to feel confident and sure of who she is. I can't, but God can! I meet so many moms who suffer from low self-esteem, low self-image, a lack of self-confidence. But how can this be if you are in Christ? If you belong to the powerful God of the universe? Is He not enough to give you courage and confidence? I love this benediction in Jude 24: "Now to Him who is able to keep you from stumbling, and to present you faultless before the presence of His glory with exceeding joy, to God our Savior, who alone is wise, be glory and majesty, dominion and power, both now and forever." *That's* the confidence you have in Christ, my friend.

> *Why do I doubt my value, Jesus? I have You*
> *and Your confidence as my very foundation!*
> *I will stand sure in Your presence and believe*
> *that I am loved. In You, I have all that I need.*

God's Exit Promise

Temptation is tricky. We feel guilty for being tempted, and then we feel unworthy to ask God for help. When you're tempted to yell at your children or keep secrets from your spouse, God has a promise for you in 1 Corinthians 10:13: "No temptation has overtaken you except such as is common to man; but God is faithful, who will not allow you to be tempted beyond what you are able, but with the temptation will also make the way of escape, that you may be able to bear it." This is God's "exit" promise. When you are tempted, He will provide a way out. The temptation itself isn't the sin—yielding to it is! God will provide *what* you need, and *when* you need it. Rest in this promise, and flourish in its power.

*God, lead me out of my temptation. It pulls
me away from Your purpose. It fogs my mind
when I want to be a faithful and diligent mom.
Thank You for giving me the power and strength
to release this temptation once and for all.*

An Incredible Gift

can't face myself—much less face God. How can He ever forgive me?" When Jesus said on the cross, "It is finished," it was finished! For your sins and mine. God's forgiveness is complete when you accept that Jesus died for your sins. *Every* sin. And this forgiveness is permanent because Jesus' work is permanent.

And the truth gets better and better. God not only forgives each sin, but He *forgets* it. As Psalm 103:12 tells us: "As far as the east is from the west, so far has He removed our transgressions from us." You're not supposed to go around messing up because of this assurance. But when you do sin, you can know God has already forgiven you. Share this incredible gift with your children and with everyone you encounter this week.

God, thank You for Your mercy. I pray that
I will walk a path of faith with my eyes on
You and my heart set in Your ways. Guide
my parenting. Help me raise children
who respect the great gift of forgiveness.

Your Behavior Is Showing

If you want to see some changes in your marriage, today's your chance for a new start. There was a time when I had to make changes because my marriage wasn't working. Oh, I was working at it, but that wasn't enough. Once I looked at some of my behavior, I could see the problems pretty clearly. I gave negative responses to Jim's ideas without even thinking about his suggestions or my response. I'd raise my voice without noticing. But Jim noticed! So I wrote down each problem behavior on a page in my prayer notebook entitled *resolutions*. Then I prayed every day for change. Slowly, that began to take place. As Paul said in Ephesians 4:24, I was to "put on the new self, created to be like God" (NIV). I encourage you to look at how you behave. You'll be glad you did. And so will your husband and your children.

God, what behaviors do I need to change? How am I impacting my family in negative ways? Show me. And give me a receptive, tender heart that is willing to embrace true transformation.

Prayer—that Again!

❧

Why is a prayer life difficult to nurture? I can think of a bunch of reasons why it's easy not to pray. For one thing, it's an exercise that requires discipline. Just the word *discipline* can make you tired. Or you think you're too busy to take the time to pray. Also, many moms who do pray regularly struggle with boredom. They say the same things over and over again, and prayer becomes more about routine than a relationship.

Please don't miss out on entering God's presence with joy and receiving the blessing of true relationship with your Lord. Ephesians 3:20 says God "is able to do exceeding abundantly above all that we ask or think." Set a goal for yourself. Commit to five minutes a day in prayer. You can do that! Then take Philippians 4:6 to heart and "let your requests be made known to God."

Jesus, I come to You today to be in Your presence, to listen, to speak, to listen again. To be the mom and woman I want to be, I need You and Your hope.

Grace

When you allow God's grace to control you in difficult times, He'll give you strength that you never knew you had. The apostle Paul said to the Christians at Corinth that they would experience weaknesses, insults, distresses, persecutions, and difficulties, but they were to take cheer because God is in control. Here's an acrostic that can help you as a mom to quickly tap into the way of grace—

Give thanks to God for His grace.
Respond in love and obedience.
Ask God for wisdom to understand what His grace means in your life and relationships.
Commune with other believers in a Bible-teaching church.
Extend God's grace to others by sharing the gospel and showing forgiveness.

Let God's sweet grace work in your heart and life. You'll be amazed at its strength and power.

Father, my hardships will not defeat me because I reside in Your grace. Let me pass it on to my husband, kids, and to all who need to hear of Your tender mercies.

You Are a Treasure

You have great value as a godly mom. You are a teacher, caregiver, nurturer, comforter, and blessing for your family. And the Bible says that if you're a godly wife, you are your husband's greatest asset. I know that on a daily basis you might not feel that way. Maybe you don't meet your own expectations in fulfilling your role as a wife. Or maybe your husband doesn't tell you he values you. But that doesn't change this truth: When you commit your way to God, you are a treasure.

Because of your character, humility, wisdom, and faithfulness, the Bible says your husband "will have no lack of gain" (Proverbs 31:11). And why is that? It's as Proverbs 31:10 states: "Who can find a virtuous wife? For her worth is far above rubies." How's *that* for success?

> *God, let me be a great treasure to my husband, family, and You. Keep my ways godly, honorable, and noble so that I am a source of spiritual wealth and a wealth of encouragement to those I love.*

Trust in the Lord

Trust in the Lord with all your heart. It's easy to cry "Yes!" when you read this in the Bible, but it's not so easy to do, is it? So can you build that trust? Double "Yes!" By depending on God, trusting Him, and relying totally on His wisdom, just as it says in Proverbs 3:5: "Trust in the LORD with all your heart, and lean not on your own understanding." It's tempting to want to take things into your own hands, yet the Bible says, "Don't be wise in your own eyes" (verse 7). Look to God's will—always! He will make your paths straight. Solomon said, "In all your ways acknowledge Him" (verse 6). Wise advice.

God will guide you into accomplishing His purposes and not your own. As you trust Him, you will become more like the Master—and more like a mom after God's own heart.

This time I mean it. I want to trust in You, Lord, with all of my heart and soul. When my leap of faith requires going out of my comfort zone and beyond my limited vision of what can be, I will trust You to carry me and to guide me.

There Is Hope

Do you feel like life is crumbling apart? Are you facing troubles with your kids or with your work? Does despair creep up on you when you allow yourself time to think? I have encouragement for you: There is hope, and you can look to God for it.

Corrie ten Boom was a prisoner in a Nazi concentration camp. No one needed hope more than she did. She said, "Never be afraid to trust an unknown future to a known God." Because of Jesus Christ, you know your future. It's one of hope. The next time you're worrying about circumstances you can't control, pray. Everything is in God's hands. Make your concern a matter of prayer and experience the blessing expressed in Romans 15:13: "May the God of hope fill you with all joy and peace in believing." Abound in hope!

> *God, I can build up daily problems into*
> *monumental ones. I must rest in Your*
> *hope each morning, each evening, and*
> *every moment in between. Today I give*
> *to You my specific worries about my family,*
> *and I accept Your peace in return.*

From Gloomy to Joyful

❦

Coming to Christ made a *big* difference in my marriage—and in *me* as a wife! I wasn't a Christian until I was nearly 29 years old. Jim and I had been married for 8 years. Jim was a Christian, so you can imagine the discussions, disagreements, and misunderstandings we had about "religion." Those were volatile years, to say the least. But the transformation of my heart, mind, and behavior when I accepted Christ was amazing! And it was instantaneous. Hope filled my heart for my life, my marriage, and my view of parenting. God's peace covered me, and I no longer worried about the future. The gloom I brought to my marriage was replaced with light and joy. Dear friend, blessings flow when you know and trust the Lord. Give Him your heart. Give Him your life.

Father, I lay my life before You today.
I'm ready and willing to step forth in the
fullness of Your grace. I want the peace
that replaces fear. I want Your joy to fill me
and my home. Transform me, Father.

The Bible—a Great Place to Be

If you're looking for a good place to spend your time, God's Word is a great place to be! You are never wasting your time if you're spending it in God's Word. Do you need wisdom? Encouragement? Strength? Direction? Forgiveness? There are endless reasons to come to the refuge of Scripture.

Hebrews 4:12 describes the Bible as "living and powerful," "sharper than any two-edged sword." When you meditate on God's Word, it speaks to your heart. It points to behaviors and attitudes that may not match up with God's standard for you. Let God's Word teach you! Martin Luther said, "The Bible is alive, it speaks to me; it has feet, it runs after me; it has hands, it lays hold on me." God wants you to live your life fully.

Lord, I skim Your Word when I should be going to it daily for my power and hope for living, parenting, growing, and loving. Teach me. And give me wisdom to teach my children where they can always find Your truth.

Is that Your Alarm?

Are you willing to start your day with the Lord? I must warn you that if you get serious about this discipline, it'll change your life. Your schedule. Your priorities. Your focus. Your perspective. Everything! But to begin, you must manage your days to make time for the pursuit of God's heart. For many busy moms, the only way to enjoy time with God is to set the morning alarm 30-45 minutes earlier. There's a reward that David talks about in Psalm 19:10. He says you'll not only hunger and thirst for more time with the Lord, but God's Word will become "sweeter also than honey and the honeycomb." Make God's Word your passion. You'll never be the same!

Jesus, I like to be in control. But things aren't working my way. I'm overly busy, impatient with the kids, and caught up in trivial matters. I hear the alarm sounding...and I'm ready to be transformed in and by Your presence.

There's Always God

God knows what He's doing. He isn't awaiting instruction from us. But that cannot be your excuse for not praying. Because God loves a relationship with you, He tells you to call on Him and to seek Him. Many moms feel they don't have anyone to talk to who *really* gets them. They spend so much time with little ones that they rarely talk about matters of the heart. Yet when it seems there's no one to talk to—and even when there is—God is ready to listen. And He gets you.

Hebrews 13:5 says the Lord will never leave you or forsake you. There's no one else you can say that about, is there? Enjoy the privilege of talking with your heavenly Father, and then wait for His answers and actions on your behalf.

Lord, You know the deepest part of me. You know my sorrows and troubles, and You know my future. Thank You for loving me and welcoming me into Your presence with a listening heart.

Now's the Perfect Time

Now's the perfect time to remind yourself of God's amazing grace. Thoughts of God's goodness and mercy will keep you humble, grateful, and worshipful all day long. And God's grace is sufficient—sufficient and sustaining for your entire day and life! It means you'll never face a trial with your child, a struggle in your marriage, or a confrontation at work that you can't handle with God's strength.

When finances are low, God's grace is sufficient. When a loved one battles a health problem, God's grace is sufficient. When a child suffers, His grace is there. You can walk in the Spirit, filled with God's love, joy, peace, patience, self-control, and wisdom, no matter what comes your way. God promises it!

Lord, I fall short when I try to fix my troubles or solve my problems. I can't make everything easy for my child. And I can't cure illness. But I can come to You and lean into Your loving, sufficient grace.

Five Revolutionary Words

Five words revolutionized my life! Those words? "Never major on the minors." They launched a complete spiritual makeover in my life that continues to this day. I evaluate every decision, activity, and minute by that wise standard. Prayerfully I ask, "Father, does this fit into your plan for me? Will this help me become a better woman by using my gifts and abilities? Does this contribute to the good of others? Is it worthy of my time?"

How do you spend *your* time? It's a question you need to ask yourself every now and then. It's amazing how bogged down you can get in the least important, least spiritual, or least meaningful aspects of life. Let those five simple and revolutionary words of wisdom shape how you live today and the days to follow.

> *Jesus, hold me back from focusing energy,*
> *worry, and my precious days on concerns*
> *of minor importance. Give me Your*
> *eternal perspective so I major on the*
> *majors—to begin with, my husband, my*
> *children, and the pursuit of Your will.*

Energy Plus

Do you live a life that builds energy? Here's a little checklist to help you evaluate the answer: Do you need to take off a few pounds? Exercise a little more? Make better food choices? Break an addictive habit? Get to bed earlier? I could go on, but you know the list. Every woman knows the list! And you understand that whether you're meeting with the Lord early in the morning, taking care of your family, or serving in a ministry, that health, energy, and stamina are essential.

I pray, and I boldly ask God for a healthy body. And with that act of diligence comes more discipline, determination, and dedication. Ask for what you need from the Lord, then live in the promises He is fulfilling in you daily.

God, give me a healthy body, mind, and
spirit. Help me embrace habits that
strengthen and energize me. I want to model
a life of balance, a faith of conviction, and a
commitment to wholeness for my children.

One Day—that's It!

All you have is one day—*today*! Sometimes you may act like time is unlimited, but you as a mom know better than anyone how days blur into years. Your children change right before your eyes. Let this be a reminder for you to live one day at a time. One small step you can take is to regularly ask these questions: (1) What is God's plan and purpose for my life? (2) What do I want to have accomplished with my life? (3) How do I want my life to have helped others? (4) What do I want to leave behind?

Ask God for insight and clarification about the answers. And speak the prayer request Psalm 90:12 presents: "Teach us to number our days, that we may gain a heart of wisdom."

God, today matters. My choices matter. There isn't time to waste. In each moment, help me to see all that it is and all that it can be when it is given over to Your hands.

Want a Better Life?

So you want a better life? I've got good news for you! Start with Philippians 3:12: "Not that I have already obtained all this, or have already arrived at my goal, but I press on to take hold of that for which Christ Jesus took hold of me" (NIV). You are to persevere and embrace what Jesus has taken hold of for you.

Here's a prayer from Psalm 39:4: "LORD, make me to know my end, and what is the measure of my days, that I may know how frail I am." You are a vulnerable being. You will be hurt. You already have scars. But there is a better life for you when you take hold of God's promises and your victory in Christ. Then, my dear friend, you will know all you need to know about the good life and your future.

Jesus, You have done all that needs to be done for my future. You shape a better life for me and my family because You direct us in Your will and You lead us to eternity.

Never Rushed

Moms juggle schedules that would make most business people sweat! Thank goodness you have the life of Jesus for inspiration. Jesus exemplifies, more than anyone else, the picture of a busy person. Yet He never seemed to be in a hurry. He was never rushed and never breathless. He continued moving purposefully through His schedule and His day. And He took time with people.

How was He able to do this? Jesus knew His priorities. Do you want to simplify your life? Determine God's priorities for you and your family. Then your schedule will fall into place. I love Paul's encouragement in 1 Corinthians 15:58: "My beloved brethren, be steadfast, immovable, always abounding in the work of the Lord, knowing that your labor is not in vain in the Lord."

*Jesus, let me be steadfast in the pursuit of
Your priorities. Help me pause during a
crazy day to listen to my child tell a story.
Let me listen intently to my husband. And
may I pay attention to the person in need.*

God's Four Words for Wives

Marriage, a good one, takes work. Hard work. And an abundance of patience. It takes commitment. It takes determination. And it takes time! I don't know about you, but whenever anything's wrong between Jim and me, I'm miserable. And when a mom is miserable, her children feel it. So what does God expect from a mom? I use what I call God's Four Words for Wives. Look up these verses and embrace God's Word for you. (1) Help your husband (Genesis 2:18). (2) Follow your husband's leadership. Maybe it's not popular, but it's right! (Ephesians 5:22). (3) Respect your husband (Ephesians 5:33). (4) And Titus 2:4 says to love your husband.

Help him, follow him, respect him, love him. Make these four "words" into four lifetime goals for you and your marriage. It'll be more than worth it!

> *God, with Your help, I can strengthen my*
> *marriage and the foundation my children*
> *call home. You give me the guidance to move*
> *forward as a godly wife and mom when*
> *I live out the four words You have for me.*

Totally Unmerited

Have you ever done something really bad—something *everyone* knew was wrong—yet they forgave you anyway? Then you know what grace is all about! God's mercy. It's God's favor—unmerited! Hear Nehemiah's prayer of thanksgiving to God for His grace to the nation Israel: "In Your great mercy You did not utterly consume them nor forsake them; for You are God, gracious and merciful" (9:31).

What about you? Ephesians 2:8 says, "By grace you have been saved through faith, and that not of yourselves; it is the gift of God." It's God's intentional loving favor for you. You can't earn it. The only way to receive it is by faith in Jesus Christ. As a mom who delights in God's salvation, you'll experience God's amazing, all-sufficient, and transforming grace!

> *Lord, when I reflect back on my life, I see so many times that You protected me, saved me from myself, led me toward Your will, and forgave me. Today—and every day—I want to express gratitude to You for my children, my faith, and my blessed life.*

Our Money Isn't Ours

You are to be a steward of everything in your life, including your finances. And like most moms, you probably have to stretch your budget! But whether you have a lot or a little, you are to follow God's giving guidance. First, you need to know what Job 1:21 underscores—that any money you have is not yours, it's God's. Then you need to stand firm in the principle of Matthew 25:23: If you are faithful with a few things, much more will be given. Giving gives back in many ways.

What do you have that God has given you? What will you do with it? The bottom line is God will take care of every area of your life. Be faithful with what He's given you already! And praise Him for all that He has yet to give.

Lord, I tend to hold back on giving when
I get afraid. But I realize that fear has no
place in a life of faith. Help me to be a
consistent, gracious giver even when resources
are limited. And I'm counting on You to
direct me how, when, and where to give.

Made for Relationship

There's no doubt that contentment—especially in the area of relationships—is a tough one! It's natural to get frustrated with our kids and become critical of our husbands. But God makes it clear in 1 Timothy 6:6 that "godliness with contentment is great gain." It's the greatest blessing you can enjoy in this world. But contentment can seem like something only other people have. However, there is hope in the apostle Paul's encouragement in Philippians 4:11: You're to *learn* to be content! This should help you to think in terms of "just enough." Just enough wealth to support your needs. Just enough strength to battle your difficulties. Just enough patience. Just enough love and faith and hope. Contentment isn't about you—it's about God in you!

Father, You know how impatient I get with my family. Grant me peace of mind and spirit so that I walk, work, love, and live in a state of contentment. I'm so grateful for all of my relationships. Give me a kind and joyful heart.

Good Steward Smarts

Money. It causes many headaches, but it is also one of life's necessities. As a mom you can benefit from becoming a wise, godly steward of your money. First, consider this powerful insight from Proverbs 22:7: "The borrower is servant to the lender." There's no freedom in debt. Rather, there's a lot of worry and risk. So now is the time to use your good steward smarts. Make a list of everything you spend your money on for one month. Then decide which expenses you can eliminate, and which ones you can reduce. As you create your new list of spending priorities, pray about it. Doing this works! When you take charge of your finances, you and your family will experience the joy of a long-forgotten freedom.

God, do not let me define my worth by
a dollar sign. Give me the good sense to
be a wise and godly steward. Lead me to
give, save, and spend in ways that honor
You and serve the needs of my family.

A True Friend

What makes a true friend? You may have your personal list, but it's best to understand what God wants so that you can be a good friend *and* seek to be one too. A true friend supports your commitments and responsibilities—in other words, your busy life and your family. She helps you with your priorities. And when you honor the Lord in your life, she rejoices right along with you! A true friend will pray with you and for you. She'll encourage you…and confront you in love when it's necessary. When you are a friend, it is important to do as Luke 6:35 says: "Do good…without expecting to get anything back" (NIV). And what is it we say? It takes a friend to be one!

> *Jesus, I turn to You as my friend in life and*
> *faith. Help me demonstrate the qualities*
> *You say are most important in a friendship.*
> *And guide me toward relationships with*
> *women who are godly and gracious.*

The Renewing of Your Mind

One of the greatest treasures I own is the "storehouse" of verses I've memorized over the years. Do you want a portable treasury of God's wisdom? Choose some verses to memorize. You'll be so glad you did. It helps immensely when teaching your children, offering advice to a friend, and setting priorities for your life. When you commit God's Word to memory, you embed it deeply into your life. Romans 12:2 encourages us to "not be conformed to this world, but be transformed by the renewing of your mind, that you may prove what is that good and acceptable and perfect will of God." When your mind is renewed, your behaviors, choices, life, and sense of purpose will follow.

Renew me, Lord! As a mom and as Your child, I want to hold the treasures of Your Word in my heart and mind so that I am never without Your comfort and leading.

Let's Get Started

When you seek examples of ways to give and serve, it's natural to look to your peers. They can be inspiring. But, mom, there are also women you encounter in the Bible who will encourage you with their use of resources and service. You can serve through hospitality like Martha and Mary, the sisters who hosted Jesus and the disciples in their home. Or you could build a prayer ministry. In Acts 12:12 the mother of John Mark held a prayer meeting at her house, where everyone prayed for Paul's release from prison. And I love the picture in 1 Timothy 5 of the widows who helped raise orphans and nurse the sick. These women are no different from you. Be inspired…and get started.

God, I love delving into the Bible and discovering how You empower women. My confidence and purpose are encouraged. I want to minister to my husband, children, family, friends, and others in whatever ways You beckon my heart.

We're in It for Life

Are your children grown up or close to leaving the nest? Take heart! This will be a time of great renewal, mom. You're just getting started! Regardless of your age or stage in life, there's no retiring from serving God. It's easy to say, "Let someone else do it. It's someone else's time to serve." The truth is that because you're bought with a price and redeemed by Jesus Christ, you are to serve passionately for life! There are younger women who would love to serve alongside an older mentor. There are new moms who desperately need the comfort and advice of a woman who has also been through 2:00 a.m. feeding times. What you can offer to others right now matters!

Good Shepherd, lead me into this new stage of life with a renewed sense of courage and conviction. I want to keep being a mom after Your heart.

Robbers in Your Life

Don't let sneaky "time robbers" deprive you of a precious day to live out God's plan and purpose. Without reviewing where your time goes, you won't know how to change your schedule for you and your family. What are you putting off that you know you should do? What is getting minimal effort or energy from you that should be getting your full attention?

If you don't plan your day, someone else will do it for you. Your kids and others will provide plenty of distractions and their version of what is priority. But don't live someone else's day. Psalm 118:24 says, "This is the day the Lord has made; we will rejoice and be glad in it." Live the day God has given you to serve Him—the one He planned for you.

Lord, I want to turn my attention and my heart toward what matters in Your sight. Give me Your discernment and perspective so that I fully experience the precious gift I have of living in Your will and living out Your purpose.

Out of Whack

Even when your goals and priorities are firmly in place, life can get out of whack. So what's a busy mom to do? Priorities are good. You'll never hear me say differently! But that doesn't mean we always manage them well. Don't let busyness make your efforts and gifts ineffective. You can easily get caught up in doing all the wrong things—and with good intentions, at that. As a result, you struggle to give your heart to the priorities God has given you.

What can you do? Pray over your priorities. Keep lifting up your needs as you shape a schedule. Prayer makes such a difference—and so will you when your day's priorities align with God's will.

Lord, what is Your will for me at this time
of my life? How can I better live out Your
plan for today and tomorrow? I don't
want to be out of whack! I want to get
on track with You—and stay there.

A No-calorie Diet

Let me ask you two questions: First, how often do you eat? Most of us eat three meals a day. Or if you're a mom of younger ones, you probably eat bits and pieces, here and there, throughout the day when you get the chance. And second, do you turn to the Bible for your *spiritual food*?

Here's my challenge: Read your Bible every day for nourishment. To get started, read one chapter in the Gospels daily, and you'll read through the life of Christ in three months. What a wealth of knowledge, information, and direction you'll have for your life—and it's just a chapter a day! You can do that. First Peter 1:24-25 says, "The grass withers, and its flower falls away, but the word of the LORD endures forever." Be wise. You are what you eat! And blessing upon blessing, God's Word contains no calories.

*Lord, You provide for all of my physical
and spiritual needs. Thank You for
the nourishment of Your Word and for
how it feeds my heart and soul.*

A Child's Prayers

P raying is intimidating. After all, it's God who hears my lame prayers!" I used to feel the same way. But I've discovered prayer isn't intimidating when your heart and intentions are right. God doesn't care so much about *how* you pray. He's not listening for flowery words. No, He's more concerned that you *do* pray! When your son or daughter comes to you with a skinned knee or a broken heart, you don't judge how they make their request for help. You're positively *glad* to show love and nurture.

And you know what? God wants to bless you and grant your requests—He wants to give what Matthew 7:11 calls "good things." And Matthew 7:7 says, "Ask, and it will be given to you; seek, and you will find; knock, and it will be opened to you." Go ahead! Get serious about prayer, and watch God answer.

Father, You hear the prayers of Your child.
This child. Thank You for listening through my
stumbles and fumbles on my way to making
my requests and my praises known. I love You.

If You Want to Grow

I f you want to grow spiritually, look for someone who's older in the faith and ask for her help. Don't wait! When I first accepted Christ I was very excited, but I knew so little. I was baffled about how to live out my faith as a mom and wife. A mentor was exactly what I needed!

There were several women who were so patient with me, who encouraged me in my spiritual growth. To this day, I'm so grateful to them. I often use the words Paul wrote in Romans 1:14 to express my gratitude: "I am a debtor" to these loving saints. Don't give up until you find that woman who fits your need for a spiritual mentor. Ask others to help you…and help you find the right person. Then continue your wonderful journey of becoming a mom after God's own heart. I'm right there with you, cheering you on!

Show me the way, God. You have someone in mind for me. Help me to trust Your timing. Give me a heart that is hungry so that I am ready to learn from another woman of God. I want to grow!

What's On for Today?

"What will I do today?" That's a great question to ask yourself! I thought about what my response would be, especially in light of wanting to be a godly mom. My next question: Who could I model my faith after today? The Bible says Enoch walked in daily fellowship with His heavenly Father. Abraham trusted implicitly in God. How about Job? He was patient under extreme circumstances. How can it get worse than losing everything? Andrew desired to lead others to Christ. Paul forgot the past and pressed forward. Proverbs 16:3 says, "Commit your works to the LORD, and your thoughts will be established." And so will your actions.

Go ahead. Ask yourself again: "What will I do *today*?"

Lord, there are remarkable men and women of the Bible who show me how to live out faith and the character and strength of a godly mom. Fill me with Your hope and courage so that I embrace today with heart and mind, and make it count.

Don't Lose Your Mind

I don't want to oversimplify this, but how we use our mind is our choice. To decide to use your mind to know God, learn His Word, study His truths, and trust His promises requires perseverance and discipline. Living out God's plan for your life requires that you use godly thinking, wisdom, and guidelines. Matthew speaks to that very issue in 12:34: "Out of the abundance of the heart the mouth speaks." The question is, "What abounds within you?" And I'm asking myself that same question. If you want to live a godly life, you have to put things in your mind that are godly. The Bible says that the peace of God will guard your heart and mind through Christ (Philippians 4:7). Seek God. Seek His peace. And give your thoughts to God's control and influence. Bless your family today. Feed your mind; don't lose it!

Jesus, Your peace is like nothing else. It is everything. Protect my heart and mind so that I can walk in my purpose as a mom who speaks out of the abundance of a godly heart.

The Weight Battle

Is every woman on a diet? Most moms vow to lose their "baby weight" after the first child. Then the second. Or third. But it's easy to delay this priority of our health because we're tired and busy. What can we do?

First Corinthians 10:31 says, "Whether you eat or drink, or whatever you do, do all to the glory of God." What does this look like? Eat only when hungry. Try this: Eat only *after* you pray. Prayer burns calories. Okay, it doesn't; but it's always good to pray! Eat half-portions. Use small plates. Eat what's healthy. And give God this area of your life so *you* can stop giving the thought of food so much energy and importance. I pray you and I can be vibrant, healthy moms.

God, take my worries over weight and food,
my guilt and shame, my bad habits, and my
past dieting failures. May I glorify You by
making healthy choices for myself and my
family when cooking, serving, and eating food.

Prayer Makes a Difference

If you wonder whether prayer works, if the act of praying does anything, let me reassure you, friend. Prayer *does* make a difference. It makes your heart pliable. Do you want a soft heart? A generous, loving, outgoing heart that gives God glory? There's no question that if you want God's leading in your decisions, parenting, relationships, and purpose, prayer is the answer. It's through prayer that you open your heart and life to God. And when you do, He searches you, exposes your motives, heals you, and guides you.

I can't imagine a life without prayer, a *day* without prayer. And believe me, I was a big skeptic! Prayer turned my life around, and God will do the same for you.

Look at my heart, Lord. Search it. You know me so well. I want to be receptive to Your Word and will. I want to be a praying woman—a praying mom! Give me a heart that perseveres in prayer.

Boring? No Way

The Bible says as Christian women we're to be temperate. But nowhere in God's Word have I read we're to be boring! My friend, it's quite the opposite. All God wants for us is a vibrant life in Christ. A fulfilling, joyous glorifying of Him in everything we are and do. I've found it to be an amazing adventure, and you will too.

Proverbs 3:9 instructs you to honor the Lord with the "firstfruits" of all you've been given and of yourself. The promised result is that you will be "filled with plenty"—overflowing, in fact! (verse 10). You'll be blessed in your spirit and your life when you give everything you are to God. It's a fulfillment and adventure that lasts more than a lifetime. There's *nothing* boring about being a mom after God's own heart.

*Jesus, take me on this adventure. I want to leap
with faith. Jump with Your joy. Parent in Your
power. And with every surprise, twist, and turn,
I want to believe in Your supernatural provision.*

Run the Race

Managing your life is like running a marathon. It's long obedience in the same direction. In 2 Timothy 4:7 Paul likens the Christian life to a race. He says "I have fought a good fight, I have finished the race, I have kept the faith." What a statement to be able to make at the end of your life—"I have kept the faith." The Christian life is certainly not a sprint to the finish line. It's much more about going the distance—at a long, sustained, steady pace. It's being steadfast, immovable, always abounding in grace" (1 Corinthians 15:58). It calls for discipline of life and soul. Isaiah 40:31 says you will "mount up with wings like eagles...run and not be weary." What mom doesn't want to hear that she won't be weary?

*God, You make a way for me and direct me
to go on and on in grace and to keep the pace.
I will rely on Your strength so that I can go the
distance and keep my faith every step of the way.*

Change Your Approach

I'm so irritated by people who don't do the right thing. I want to shout at them to shape up!" Let's face it, we've all been tempted to do the same. But it isn't for you to oversee what other people do or don't do. However, training up your kids *is* your job, but parenting everyone else around is not! There's enough of your own "stuff" to work on. Concern yourself with what God wants for you and from you.

God wants to work through you in the lives of your family and others with love, maturity, and a passion for His glory. He desires to conform you to the image of your Savior, so that He will be glorified by your behavior. That's a different standard than the one the world gives you, isn't it? Let your life mirror the characteristics of your heavenly Father.

*Father, turn my attention to what I can do
about my behavior, my kids, and my purpose.
Give me a heart of love for others so that my life
reflects Your grace at home and to the world.*

The Best Choices

We've all made bad decisions in the past. The good news is that we can start making good decisions with God's leading. John 15:10 quotes Jesus as saying, "If you keep My commandments, you will abide in My love, just as I have kept My Father's commandments and abide in His love."

Be a woman who walks with God and a mom who makes decisions based on God's wisdom. Read your Bible—do it every day. Join a Bible study if that'll help you. And pray! Do that every moment. Your waking prayer each morning should be that you make choices that honor God and His Word. What's the point? To help you make good choices…better choices…the *best* choices!

Lord, I don't want to carry around this mental
list of bad decisions I've made. I'm ready to
leave them in the past and commit myself
to making better choices, the best choices, in
the freedom of Your amazing grace.

Joy Is Better

Joy is a whole lot better than happiness. Here are three reasons why: (1) Joy is permanent. It's rooted in an unchanging God. And as you walk in the Spirit, the Holy Spirit *produces* joy! (2) Joy is always available. It's based on a faithful God. Philippians 4:4 reminds us to "rejoice in the Lord always." Whatever your circumstances, rejoice! (3) Your joy is inexpressible. Peter described this in 1 Peter 1:8: "Though now you do not see Him, yet believing, you rejoice with joy inexpressible and fully of glory."

Happiness can fade the moment your child refuses to eat his breakfast...or sooner! But you have ready access to the source of true joy—a joy that no one can take away from you. So reach out and take hold of the joy that is yours forever.

> *Lord, You are my giver of joy and all*
> *things good. Thank You for a peace*
> *and a delight that surpasses the daily,*
> *circumstantial rise and fall of happiness.*

Every Step and Breath

If today is "one of those days" for you, I want you to know God is available to you *every* moment—no matter what you're dealing with! Do what you're doing. Focus on God. Find your joy in Him, true joy in His promises. Ask Him for grace. Ask Him to help you remember to go to Him in these times of need for His filling. Until we're with the Lord, there will always be suffering, disappointment, dashed dreams, even ridicule and persecution. But let it cause you to offer Him a sacrifice of praise and allow you to be touched by Him. James 1:2 reminds us to "count it all joy when you fall into various trials, knowing that the testing of your faith produces patience." Praise Him with every step and breath!

God, before I place my feet on the floor in the morning, I will dedicate my day to You. I will commit to making a difference for my kids and for others. And I will count it joy to have Your strength to stand on when trials come my way.

No Matter What, We're Blessed

When a well-known newspaper counselor was asked what one problem stood out among the thousands of questions she received, she said, "Fear!" You probably guessed that. We all face it, don't we? We're surrounded by fear. But here's the good news for us as believers in Christ: We have a built-in antidote to fear. It's the peace of God. It's possible to experience peace in a crazy, hectic world—or even a crazy, hectic household. Philippians 4:7 calls this the kind of peace "which surpasses all understanding." And here's some good news. You can possess it right in the middle of your trials, when you need it the most. Wow—let that truth sink into your heart!

Oh, Jesus, You bless me in abundance.
You refresh my spirit and ease my pain.
Why do I let fear creep into my heart?
Give me Your peace and perspective so that
I look beyond fear to the blessing of Your peace.

Pray, Pause, and Peruse

So you've got kids and you want a little peace and quiet. Here are three P's—the steps to getting there: pray, pause, and peruse! *Pray* first, pray often, and pray continually. Place all those concerns you have stored up in your mind into God's hands. Then *pause* and turn to the Lord when a crisis or disaster comes along. If your child falls ill. If you get notice that your company is downsizing. God promises to never leave you nor forsake you. The last P is *peruse*. Peruse God's Word. Study Jesus' life. Notice the peace He experienced in the midst of very stressful situations. Carry Jesus' attitude in your mind in whatever you do today or any day. Pray. Pause. Peruse. Allow your heart to rest in Him and experience His peace—even in your most difficult challenge!

> *God, You know the hardship I'm*
> *facing. I ask for Your mighty peace to fill*
> *me. I ask for Your covering and strength*
> *so that I see Your hand in this situation.*
> *I praise You for Your tender mercies.*

Griping and Complaining

I'm sure you've held a pity party for one. Like me, you probably thought griping would accomplish something because, for a brief moment, you let off some steam. But soon you discovered that what *works* isn't always what's *best*. I have to admit sometimes I find myself blurting out, "No way. I don't want to follow through on that responsibility again." Then I go on my way, doing what I have to do, on my own, by my own power—griping and complaining as I do. When you experience times like these, you need to follow the Lord's example. You need to pray. You need to turn to the Father and grapple with your heart until you realize that God's attitude is love, joy, and peace. I know because this is what I learned...the hard way. As a mom who encourages the spiritual maturity of your kids, you need to spend the time, however long it takes, to allow God to fill you with His Spirit. As God's Word says, He is sufficient. He *is*!

*Forgive me, Lord. How many times have
I grumbled and moaned about a rough day
with the kids? Instead of giving voice to
my woes and letting off steam, I will praise
You and give voice to Your faithfulness.*

It's Better to Do Nothing

One of the hardest things we'll ever do is nothing. When you want to give in to your emotions and let loose with anger, stop and think and pray. Then remain silent. You can't take back harmful words spoken out of frustration to your child. So what should you do? Proverbs 19:11 says, "The discretion of a man makes him slow to anger, and his glory is to overlook a transgression." In other words, lengthen your fuse. Learn to restrain your anger. Pray for all that you need in that moment! Jesus did this very thing. First Peter 2:23 tells us Jesus entrusted Himself to God. "When they hurled their insults at him, he did not retaliate; when he suffered, he made no threats. Instead, he entrusted himself to him who judges justly" (NIV). You too can resist a spirit of retaliation and entrust yourself to God. The result? Patience prevails.

> *Jesus, You endured such humiliation and*
> *violence and yet You held back from unleashing*
> *threats. When I'm tempted to let loose with*
> *rage, let my thoughts rush to Your example*
> *so that I learn once again the way of grace.*

A Kind Mom

Who in your life is an example of kindness? If asked the same question, would your kids think of you? We think of kindness as gentleness and graciousness. But I'll take that definition one active step further: Kindness *plans* to do something. It prepares for doing good and it looks for opportunities to serve. A kind mom asks, "Who needs love today?" "Who needs care and hope?" "How can I ease my child's burden?" Kindness is tenderness and concern for other people. Second Timothy 2:24 says, "A servant of the Lord must not quarrel but be gentle to all, able to teach, patient." When you genuinely care about people, you pay attention to their circumstances and you're concerned with their welfare. Start practicing an active kindness at home. You'll be amazed at how infectious it is.

God, let me be a model of active kindness for my children. Remind me to seek opportunities to extend Your love and acceptance both at home and when interacting with others outside.

What Does Faithfulness Look Like?

Since we're ready to embrace an active faith, let's direct that commitment toward faithfulness. How can we put faithfulness in action? A mom who walks faithfully with God follows through on whatever she has to do, no matter what. She shows up for her family and others. She keeps her word. James 5:12 says, "Let your 'Yes' be 'Yes,' and your 'No,' 'No.'" Keep your commitments and be reliable—always. Be devoted to duty as Jesus was when He came to do His Father's will. I've met so many women who change their minds like the weather. This, in turn, changes their loyalties, priorities, and standards. The question to ask as a mom after God's own will is this: You can count on the Lord. But can He count on you?

Lord, may You search my heart and find me
to be faithful in my actions and thoughts. Let
me put real energy toward being faithful
as a wife, mom, and woman of God.

Creative Parenting

Do you know you're created in the image of God? I want it to sink into your heart and mind that you're a creative and intelligent woman! You are a reflection of God's glory. You reflect Him to other people, especially to your children. Every time you reach out in love, perform a deed of kindness, and show forgiveness, patience, and faithfulness, others experience the character of God through you.

Resolve to continue spending time with God on a daily basis through prayer and the study of His Word. Draw inspiration from God's heart and let the Creator help you parent through the hard times and the sweet moments. Rejoice in the strength He gives for each day, and the hope He offers for every day!

*Creator, You are with me every step of the way
in this parenting job. I am excited to share You
with my child by living out Your goodness. When
I need a boost or an attitude adjustment, Your
ever-present hope brings relief and renewal.*

A Faithful God

sure understand what it means to be my own worst enemy. Self-discipline is difficult, isn't it? I resist it even when I know I'm sabotaging God's peace and purpose in my life and home. If you're cringing at the thought of self-discipline, or your lack of it, find a way to serve our faithful God.

What is your area of unfaithfulness? Stubbornness, procrastination, gossiping? When you walk by the Spirit, trusting God to guide you at every step, you can win over anything. Take heart, for God has a pattern of victory for you at the other end of this experience. Moses praised God in Deuteronomy 32:4 and said, "He is the Rock." You'll find your strength when you stand on the firm foundation of God's might.

Lord and my Rock, give me the strength
to be disciplined where I have been
unfaithful. I don't want to undermine the
good work You are doing in my life. Thank
You for Your example of faithfulness.

No More Regrets

"My problem isn't what I do. It's what I *don't* do that frustrates me!"

You're a busy mom, right? It's easy to think of excuses not to spend time in God's Word or in prayer. "I'm too tired. I don't believe I can do it. I do enough for my kids and family." Sound familiar? This unfaithfulness can lead to apathy: "Why bother?" Or the very destructive state of rebellion that says, "I won't do it!"

Every time you choose nothing over God's "something," you're missing out on the abundant life. Proverbs 29:1 warns, "He who is often rebuked, and hardens his neck, will suddenly be destroyed, and that without remedy." Don't let this become you. Instead, experience the fullness of God's purpose for you as a mom who lives without regret!

Father, I don't want any more regrets. I pray
to be committed in my walk with You. Let me
embrace Your purpose, Your special "something"
for me. I long for the abundance of faithful living.

Thanksgiving Day Every Day

What mom hasn't dreamed of coming home to a table set with fine linens and a delicious, prepared meal? When David prayed to God in Psalm 23, he said, "You prepare a table before me" (verse 5). Your host for this feast is the Lord Himself. And the table is prepared for you in advance because you're an anticipated, invited guest!

Imagine! Your divine host is the awesome, all-powerful, all-knowing God. He is attentive, watching for every opportunity to provide for you, continually refilling your cup. He delights in pouring out a generous portion! Mom, this dream is real. God invites you to this table of fellowship, covenant, and thanksgiving.

Have a seat! Participate with Him in His personal love for you.

Relax...and enjoy!

Sweet Lord, You are so loving. So kind. My defenses fall away when I'm in Your presence. I delight in this feast and am nourished by Your attention, delight, and care.

Live by the Spirit

agree with the person who said: "If you're alive, you're tempted!" When you see a magazine cover featuring mouthwatering chocolate-frosted cupcakes, the food cravings are usually strong. And carrots just won't do! Temptation also enters your thought life regarding deeper matters. Maybe you daydream about a guy you work with? Or you are jealous of a neighbor's better house, a friend's fabulous vacation, or a mom who doesn't have to work.

Galatians 5:16 reminds us that when such thoughts, emotions, and temptations fill you, God's Spirit goes against your sinful nature. "Walk in the Spirit, and you shall not fulfill the lust of the flesh." The good news is you can claim God's power, walk by His Spirit, exercise self-control, and win the battle over temptation!

God, keep me from nurturing temptations with
daydreams, fantasies, or discussion with friends.
I want my heart to be pure so that I teach
my kids, by example, to walk in the Spirit.

Like Christ

If you want the most out of life, you've got to get your act together, get the right attitude going. Are you motivated yet? Okay, that might be a premature pep talk. So let's explore what you want out of your life. Here's a possible list: A healthy, godly family. A sense of God's purpose. A heart filled with Christ's joy. Well, dear mom, God wants you to live this life too!

First John 3:2 says, "When He is revealed, we shall be like Him." The very next verse tells us how. "Everyone who has this hope in Him purifies [herself], just as He is pure." When your hope is to be like Christ, you *are* getting the most out of life!

Lord, You want the best for me. You know
the needs of my husband, my children, and
my own heart. Give me a hunger to be
godly, and the discipline to follow through.

God Says So

Because I said so." Most moms have given this blanket explanation to their children a time or two! When they want a reason to eat their peas. When they wonder why their room has to be clean before they can play. That line, even if generic, is an expression of authority. Bottom line, sometimes it's the only answer your children need to hear.

Think about how many times God has had to state His authority so you would walk in His ways, believe His promises, accept His love, or forgive others. First Timothy 5:10 urges you as a woman to live a life that earns a reputation for good works. Doing so honors God. It honors you and your family. And it is a lasting investment. Even on days when you struggle to follow what is right, your heavenly Father has something for you to hear. You guessed it!

Father, how stubborn I can be! I ask questions.
I make excuses. I wander from Your truth.
I demand explanations. But You have authority
over my life, and You want the best for me.
I will follow Your will because You said so.

Why Grow?

🌹

"I f I charted my spiritual growth once a year like I measure my children's height, I don't think I would show much progress!" This is true for many of us during certain seasons. But we should be growing in the Lord daily. So what's holding us back? And why grow? Second Corinthians 4:16 says, "We do not lose heart. Even though our outward [woman] is perishing, yet the inward [woman] is being renewed day by day." Our physical body is getting older. But our spiritual self has the opportunity, through Christ, to always be made new.

Spiritual growth is God's goal for your life. Make it a habit each day to reaffirm God's purposes for you. Read His Word, pray, and experience the wonder of renewal.

God, I want to look back on this past
year and know that I served You, loved
You, and shared You with greater spiritual
depth, wisdom, and commitment.

Exciting, Electric, and Energizing

God's Word is exciting and energizing. It's even thrilling! Why? Because it is life-changing and heart-transforming. Today the Bible is my lifeline. For the first 28 years of my life, I turned to everything *but* the Bible for help. Ever since the day I discovered the truth about Jesus Christ in the Bible, I've relentlessly devoured His Word. My appetite for the life-giving, lifesaving, life-sustaining truths in Scripture has only increased as the years have gone by.

Proverbs 2:6 says, "The LORD gives wisdom; from His mouth come knowledge and understanding." What you read between the covers of your Bible is wisdom for all your trials and for eternity. Stand on it. Live by it. And teach it to your children every day so that they too have the thrill of a transformed life.

Lord, Your Word leads me to the refuge
of Your heart. It fills me with passion
to love You and compassion for loving
my children. Transform me, Lord.

Joy When Everything's Going Wrong

When you face a hardship, praise and thanksgiving and happy thoughts don't flow too easily, do they? That's when you must deliberately choose to follow God's advice in 1 Thessalonians 5:18 and "in everything give thanks." If that faith assignment still seems tough, think of joy and thanksgiving as your way of making Hebrews 13:15 come true in your life: "Let us continually offer the sacrifice of praise to God." Your obedience and thanksgiving is a *sacrifice of praise*.

You'll discover that joy is enlarged when you look beyond your pain or disappointment to what God promises as a "fruit" of His Spirit. The joy of the Lord is never dependent on circumstances, but rather, on your willingness to accept His gift.

Lord, You provide a peace and joy that surpasses
any happiness I receive from worldly pursuits
and pleasures. It is lasting and true. I give to You
my sacrifice of praise today…and each day to
follow. You are worthy, Lord, of such obedience.

Plan Time for Yourself

A mom needs time alone to recharge her battery—spiritually and physically. So devote some quiet moments with God to grow personally and spiritually. As 2 Peter 3:18 puts it: "Grow in the grace and knowledge of our Lord and Savior Jesus Christ." If you're preparing yourself to bless your family and others, and if you want to have an influence on them, plan time for yourself to be in God's Word. The only way you can make time work for you rather than becoming its slave is to plan, set, and follow through with realistic, godly priorities. Ask God to help you every step of the way. Your Father knows you need rest, instruction, comfort, strength, wisdom, grace…and lots of unconditional love! Go to Him. He will restore you.

Father, I seek the sanctuary of Your arms.
I need the balm of Your love. My time with You
restores my faith, keeps me connected to Your
heart, and reminds me of the privilege of being
a mother. I savor these moments each day.

Arranging a Bouquet

I love flowers. Years ago, as an occasional treat, I'd buy a mixed bunch at the supermarket, tear off the cellophane, and plop the flowers into a vase. Then I learned how to transform the bouquet with a little care and arranging. I began to create lovely displays of color, texture, and beauty. Life is like that, mom! Why plop a bunch of mixed activities into your day when you can arrange God's priorities with care and prayer? The result is a vibrant life of delight and meaning that brings joy to you and your husband, children, and God.

God has gifted you to live life for Him (see 2 Peter 1:3). Let your faith life become a beautiful, fragrant centerpiece. Close today by praying the heart of 2 Corinthians 2:14-15 in a personal way.

God, thank You for leading me in triumph in Christ. Through me, You diffuse the fragrance of Christ's knowledge in every place. Let me be the fragrance of Christ among those in my life starting at home. Let my life be a beautiful offering.

The Woman of Your Dreams

Are you holding on to a lifelong dream with both hands? My friend, *God* will take you as far as you want to go! Just for fun, what age are you now? And how old will you be in ten years? Now imagine what those ten years may hold. You need God's strength for the events of those years—to grow spiritually. To grow as a mom. To grow as a woman. Whatever the future holds for you, God will help you successfully serve the people in your life with His grace and in His strength. "Above all else, guard your heart, for everything you do flows from it" (Proverbs 4:23 NIV). Be the woman of your dreams. God *will* take you as far as you want to go!

Lord, You are the keeper, maker, and giver of my dreams. Don't let me give up hope. Please shape the desires of my heart to match Your purpose for my life so that I walk forward in Your will and not my own.

Favorite Scriptures

_____

_____

_____

_____

_____

_____

_____

_____

_____

_____

_____

_____

Favorite Scriptures

_____

_____

_____

_____

_____

_____

_____

_____

_____

_____

_____

_____

Favorite Truths About God

_____

_____

_____

_____

_____

_____

_____

_____

_____

_____

Favorite Insights

Books by Elizabeth George

- Beautiful in God's Eyes
- Breaking the Worry Habit…Forever
- Finding God's Path Through Your Trials
- Following God with All Your Heart
- The Heart of a Woman Who Prays
- Life Management for Busy Women
- Loving God with All Your Mind
- Loving God with All Your Mind DVD and Workbook
- A Mom After God's Own Heart
- A Mom After God's Own Heart Devotional
- Moments of Grace for a Woman's Heart
- One-Minute Inspiration for Women
- Quiet Confidence for a Woman's Heart
- Raising a Daughter After God's Own Heart
- The Remarkable Women of the Bible
- Small Changes for a Better Life
- Walking With the Women of the Bible
- A Wife After God's Own Heart
- A Woman After God's Own Heart®
- A Woman After God's Own Heart® Deluxe Edition
- A Woman After God's Own Heart®— Daily Devotional
- A Woman's Daily Walk with God
- A Woman's Guide to Making Right Choices
- A Woman's High Calling
- A Woman's Walk with God
- A Woman Who Reflects the Heart of Jesus
- A Young Woman After God's Own Heart
- A Young Woman After God's Own Heart— A Devotional
- A Young Woman's Guide to Prayer
- A Young Woman's Guide to Making Right Choices

Study Guides

- Beautiful in God's Eyes Growth & Study Guide
- Finding God's Path Through Your Trials Growth & Study Guide
- Following God with All Your Heart Growth & Study Guide
- Life Management for Busy Women Growth & Study Guide
- Loving God with All Your Mind Growth & Study Guide
- Loving God with All Your Mind Interactive Workbook
- A Mom After God's Own Heart Growth & Study Guide
- The Remarkable Women of the Bible Growth & Study Guide
- Small Changes for a Better Life Growth & Study Guide
- A Wife After God's Own Heart Growth & Study Guide
- A Woman After God's Own Heart® Growth & Study Guide
- A Woman's Call to Prayer Growth & Study Guide
- A Woman's High Calling Growth & Study Guide
- A Woman Who Reflects the Heart of Jesus Growth & Study Guide

Children's Books

- A Girl After God's Own Heart
- A Girl After God's Own Heart Devotional
- God's Wisdom for Little Girls
- A Little Girl After God's Own Heart

Books by Jim George

- 10 Minutes to Knowing the Men and Women of the Bible
- The Bare Bones Bible® Handbook
- The Bare Bones Bible® for Teens
- A Boy After God's Own Heart
- A Husband After God's Own Heart
- Know Your Bible from A to Z
- A Leader After God's Own Heart
- A Man After God's Own Heart
- A Man After God's Own Heart Devotional
- The Man Who Makes a Difference
- One-Minute Insights for Men
- A Young Man After God's Own Heart
- A Young Man's Guide to Making Right Choices

Books by Jim & Elizabeth George

- A Couple After God's Own Heart
- A Couple After God's Own Heart Interactive Workbook
- God's Wisdom for Little Boys
- A Little Boy After God's Own Heart

About the Author

Elizabeth George is a bestselling author and speaker whose passion is to teach the Bible in a way that changes women's lives. For information about Elizabeth's speaking ministry, to sign up for her mailings, or to purchase her books, visit her website:

www.ElizabethGeorge.com

Elizabeth George
P.O. Box 2879
Belfair, WA 98528